To Dorothy & Hugh,
May God bless you
richly through this
story, and may it be
a great encouragement
to your spirits.
Shannon

From Ash
to
Embers

The Odyssey and Overhaul of
an Ordinary Missionary

SK Conaghan

WESTBOW°
PRESS
A DIVISION OF THOMAS NELSON
& ZONDERVAN

Scripture quotations taken from the Holy Bible, New Living Translation, Copyright © 1996, 2004. Used by permission of Tyndale House Publishers, Inc., Wheaton, Illinois 60189. All rights reserved.

New Revised Standard Version Bible, copyright © 1989, Division of Christian Education of the National Council of the Churches of Christ in the United States of America. Used by permission. All rights reserved.

WestBow Press books may be ordered through booksellers or by contacting:

WestBow Press
A Division of Thomas Nelson & Zondervan
1663 Liberty Drive
Bloomington, IN 47403
www.westbowpress.com
1 (866) 928-1240

Because of the dynamic nature of the Internet, any web addresses or links contained in this book may have changed since publication and may no longer be valid. The views expressed in this work are solely those of the author and do not necessarily reflect the views of the publisher, and the publisher hereby disclaims any responsibility for them.

This book is a work of non-fiction. Unless otherwise noted, the author and the publisher make no explicit guarantees as to the accuracy of the information contained in this book and in some cases, names of people and places have been altered to protect their privacy.

Any people depicted in stock imagery provided by Thinkstock are models, and such images are being used for illustrative purposes only. Certain stock imagery © Thinkstock.

ISBN: 978-1-4908-6368-9 (sc)
ISBN: 978-1-4908-6367-2 (hc)
ISBN: 978-1-4908-6369-6 (e)

Library of Congress Control Number: 2014922330

Printed in the United States of America.

WestBow Press rev. date: 2/2/2015

CONTENTS

In Memory of Samuel Harrison

Whatever Happened to that Youthful Spark?

When I was a kid, I could fly. I would take the screen out of my bedroom window, crawl across the roof of our garage, and jump as far out into open air as I could. For that split second, a moment paused in time, nothing gripped me, nothing nailed me down; I was free. I was flying.

I remember the grass below as fresh, and the soil soft and forgiving. Mum had no idea at the time that I was practicing flying off our rooftop, or she would have finished the job and killed me before I accidentally killed myself.

I lived for moments when everything that tied me safely to a tether was loosed and I was free.

As a teenager, freedom gained purpose as I came to a deeper understanding of my freedom in Christ. I wanted to know that freedom in every crease of life. The impulse to tell others ignited a fire in my soul. I dreamt about remote places in the world where people had not heard that they could be free from death and sin. Praying for them kept me up late at night. I expected God to move; wanting to be part of his plan fed my spark.

At university, I discovered I was not the only one with a spark for missions. I found all-night meetings and joined other fire-filled people in prayer. I learned from them as they gave up their last bits of cash so others could eat or sleep and meet Jesus. It was freeing to be so dependent on God. The experience fanned my burning internal flame.

I went to remote places. I urged others to take a trip, hear a call, and to pray; I tried to get other spark-bearers to join me. I talked non-stop about the needs and opportunities to help people, their stories, the shortness of life, and the reality of eternity.

I had a youthful spark that burned for missions; extinguishing it seemed impossible. Some tried. They made an attempt to impress on me the more profitable and safe things I might do with my seventy-odd years on earth: get a decent-paying job, get married, settle down, have kids, make money. I was encouraged to do something, anything, other than give it all up for the sake of — there was a lot of confusion on what I'd be going over there to do.

I plodded through discouragement that often came wrapped in good intentions. Every time I felt like I could not go on, I hung on the words Jesus spoke about leaving home and giving it all up for his sake, clinging to the promise that those who do would receive a hundred times more in the end (Matt. 19:29-30, Mark 10:29-30).

Whoa. A hundred times more. Whatever that meant, it sure sounded right. I wanted in on that.

Money? I had no doubt that God would support his own work, even if it meant that I went hungry a couple days here and there. More radically, though still true, even if I died of starvation, God's provision for his work would never go amiss. When I had to raise thousands of dollars in a matter of weeks,

God gave me a faith that did not flinch; if it was meant to be, then it would be by his hand. If people asked where the money was coming from, I would say: God. Some were curious, some thought of it as daftly irresponsible. They wondered how I could just *hope* that people would give money to what I do? But I didn't hope for *people* to give, I trusted that God would provide.

I learned sadly that some Christians do not consider missionary work a valid occupation. A few commented outright that they would not be willing to pay for the satisfaction of my passing juvenile desire to travel. They were convinced the travel bug would fade and I would eventually need to settle down and get a real job. They assured me that they would not part with their godly-earned cash to pay for me to see the world. I decided then, in my mid-twenties, that I would not again ask outright for money from any one hard-working human unless I felt supernaturally prodded; I would ask God for provision. If God compelled anybody, it would be by his prompting. God provides as he chooses through willing vessels. I wanted to live joyfully, fully depending on God.

I got accused of being financially irresponsible, and worse, of having Superhero Faith. There are no real Faith Superheroes, just ordinary obedient fools with a spark that burns for missions.

I was one unstoppable fool.

******

So here I am, fifteen years later, and I feel like a delayed sloth someone put through the fast-spin cycle with a bottle of hemp-laced bleach. Whatever happened to that youthful spark that burned for missions?

Spark? I can't even find my coffee in the morning without a cup of coffee to get me to the stove to make coffee.

Youthful? Truth be told, the vibrant youth of life has passed and left me in its smouldering ashes. I grasp at a few remaining trails of wild memories as they slip between my stiff fingers. The worst part is that I don't realise it is gone and am still trying to live and act (though, not dress) like a seventeen year old. The proof is all there, though: I generally hate social media (because it feels too much like administration), A Fun Night Out is dinner with a few friends at a restaurant where the music isn't so loud you can't have a decent conversation, and my workout routine has finally taken a turn for low-impact aerobics.

As for missions, I came to a point that I would have a hard time defining what missions in this generation is if a church asked me to address the congregation about it. Most of the time, between trying to make ends meet in a lonely overseas life, updating the church with as much enthusiasm as I can muster (feign) on a quarterly basis about my seemingly less successful attempts at missions, and spreading myself thin, I lost my grip on what the point of my involvement in missions was in the first place. I felt trapped.

I always thought I was pretty lucky never to have broken any bones as a daring child. I didn't think I had, because as a frequent rooftop-jumper, I had never felt any pain, however, recent X-rays show that my ankles were cracked and fractured several times during childhood. When the doctor showed me that, dumbfounded that there was no medical record for the fractures, I had an immediate suspicion as to what might have caused those. I never felt the impact of the crash at the end of the glorious free fall; I was so full of the adrenaline rush that whatever pain I experienced on the landing was overshadowed as a kid. It caught up to me; the ground rushed up at me, and as I braced for the bone-jarring impact of burnout, I forgot about my freedom.

I *had* a youthful spark that burned for missions. Now the only things burning are my brain cells, my bank account, my candle at both ends, my ministry, my feet at the end of the day, my social life — in fact, I'm just burnt altogether: Burnt Out.

BURN ...

As a ten year old, I read a thin book called *God's Adventurer*. My Auntie Eleanor had it sent over from Northern Ireland for my birthday. I loved it. It was the story about a man who went from living his life in the certain comforts of England to taking up the new challenge of living overseas and essentially becoming as Chinese as possible; he dressed like the Chinese, learned to speak the language, ate with proper Chinese etiquette, and learned cultural customs and behaviour. He did it all with the intention of removing any obstacle that being British might present to the Chinese people. He aimed to ensure the Chinese that following Christ had nothing to do with adopting Western culture. Hudson Taylor wanted his message to be clear: the people of China have been created in love with a purpose to be restored to their Creator.

Though he died many years before I was born, Hudson Taylor was a living inspiration to me. The chalk-white Englishman dressed in traditional Chinese clothing typical to the Qing Dynasty of the mid-nineteenth century, a long train of gathered hair swinging down his back from a mostly shaven head, speaking a rounded singsong Mandarin with practiced perfection, behaving more Chinese than the Chinese youth in his presence glowed brightly in his generation. He ignited a blaze that consumed generations beyond him, even after he was long dead. His one small torch amid the Chinese spread like wildfire throughout Asia and across the waking mission force in Great Britain, Europe, and eventually North America.

As a young girl, the story burnt an indelible image on my mind. His example of what missions could look like was compelling. I knew even then that I wanted to be a missionary like J. Hudson Taylor.

I just never thought it meant I'd actually have to go to Asia.

ABSORBING ASIA

Asia took me by surprise. I sustained and eventually sanctioned a sensory onslaught that seeped into my lungs, skin, nostrils, ears, head, and heart. At first, Asia was a glittering jewel, chromed and carpeted, a bustling object of sanitised richness and beauty. That façade didn't last longer than my visit to Chiangi Airport in Singapore.

I had survived the initial twenty-hour flight and figured that if I could endure that torture, nothing could be too difficult. That became true, but only after I began to seriously pay attention to my own expectations.

Expectations are those silently unidentified and often unchallenged tagalongs who carry with them the potential to sabotage just about everything. When something or someone doesn't live up to our expectations (perhaps ones we hold without even realising) we get flustered, get our hearts broken, hopes dashed, and dreams crushed. I didn't quite realise I had so many, but the duration of that first flight to Asia quickly convinced me I was living with some serious hidden expectations. I started keeping a new journal. The first five pages were filled with expectations of what I might encounter on my whirlwind initiation to Asia, things like cockroaches and stark language barriers.

Before I contemplated personal cockroach defence tactics, though, I had to first accept that I was heading East. It had not been on my bucket list. I had never intended to go to Asia, but within three weeks, I had gone from reluctant consideration to following in the pronounced hundred year old footsteps of J. Hudson Taylor.

Just a few months prior to taking that unexpected trip, I was nearing the end of another round of education and had no idea what to do with my life. I had a blossoming dream, but the logistics didn't seem to be coming together the way I thought they should, even though it seemed to be perfect timing; I had flawlessly arranged goals, fit to what I determined to be God's Will. I couldn't figure out why God didn't agree with my expectations. Why was he making it so difficult to do what I interpreted as his instructions?

I was foolishly tied to life-on-schedule, as if God's plans were ordered by my ability to organise them into culturally defined segments. I placed faith in an ideal that was based on a very Western Evangelical perspective. It wasn't working out like I had thought it should, to say the least.

As April came around, I still didn't have a foggy clue about what to do with my life, and my graduation date was set for May. I was beginning to get antsy. One Sunday morning, a missionary from church, presented the idea of getting involved with an Asian organisation. Wayne said they were looking for someone to work in mobilising and coordinating short-term missions.

On one hand, this opportunity related to my blossoming dream in that it was missionally focused, but being missional is a whole lot different from Career Missionary. I never really saw myself working in a traditional mission organisation in traditional mission settings or in traditional ways. I had reservations, albeit flakey ones. Nonetheless, I was considering the offer.

On the other hand, I was more recently familiar with Latin, European, and African cultures and languages. The Asian mission doesn't focus in any of these areas, obviously. They are strictly and wholly all about Asia. They are *very* focused on things, people and places where I had no personal vision, I am sorry to admit. They do great work in areas where I had no interest in working. I called them reservations, but I was just closed to the idea. I had a bit of an attitude about it, too.

My initial reaction was: Gee, thanks, but I'm really not into it. It was a nice way of saying: I don't wanna.

When God invites us to enter his kingdom, and brings his ways into our world and our measly lives, there are always things we find strange and uncomfortable. His ways are not our ways. Strangely, his ways make us comfortable in their pull, like it's right where we need to be, and just what we need to be doing. I sat in that very strange uncomfortable place for about two weeks while I tried desperately to push the offer right out of my world. It was kind of like batting away at one of those rubber balls strung tightly to a paddle. The thought just kept bouncing back and hitting me in the head. I finally turned to face it and had a talk with God about the whole idea. I had all my points in order and here was how my well-presented argument went: Almighty Loving God, I really appreciate the vote of confidence in an offer like this, but: I don't speak any Asian languages, I've never been to Asia, I have no interest in going to Asia, Japanese food and I don't get along, and it is scary to address the *really* unknown Asia Factor in my cross-continental lifestyle. Thanks, but no thanks, it makes me strangely uncomfortable.

In response, I heard a simple quiet question: *My daughter, are you not willing to learn something new from me?*

Man, I would have *really* liked to say No to that.

Nonetheless, it was an invitation, not an order or a fierce command. It rarely is, is it? I was certainly welcome to decline and miss out on whatever learning opportunities might lie ahead. We are always welcome to decline. God never forces us to do anything; that is the point of free will, even within our relationship. But who says No to a question like that? Since when is this whole Follow Christ thing about making *me* comfortable? I faced the worst resistance in myself, and I laughed at silly little me.

I chose to follow.

Three weeks later, I boarded a plane and was off on the unexpected twenty-hour flight to Singapore. Comfort is strangely irrelevant when presented with the opportunity of joyfully living life to the fullest.

Singapore was only an hour-long airport stop. I found a $5 shower complete with towel and soap, marvelled at the shopping malls, game shows, massage parlours, luxury lounges, and specialty boutiques, and finally closed my mouth and connected to my Manila flight.

That's when I started writing out my new journal of expectations. I was about to stay in one of the poorest neighbourhoods in Manila. I began to pray that God would interfere with my expectations and help me deal graciously with reality. A short flight later, I stepped off the plane into Asia's metropolitan slice of Latin-Polynesian fusion. I had gone from Chiangi Airport, which felt like a pristine international fair grounds, into the swarming humidity of the Philippines. The haze was suffocating, especially in the overcrowded and heavily smog-filled city where the average low temperature is a sticky 35°C.

Asia crept along my skin. After a few hot hours under the scorching sun, amid the fog-thick pollution, pressing crowds of sweaty people in 40°C, the shirt has to be peeled from your back. A scratched arm scrapes off a layer of dirt, sweat, and sticky sunscreen. I joined the local population in the tradition of taking two cold showers daily. Or three.

I reviewed my recently started new journal of expectations. I was optimistic about learning to communicate and make friends. I had minor concerns about challenges to my emotional stamina in the heat and living conditions. Two pages were dedicated to the cockroach meet-and-greet; I had not yet reached a clear strategy, although a smash-and-dash approach was looking good.

I spent a night in Welfareville where the housing arrangement goes from basic to shockingly less than primitive. An average city block sized area houses approximately 3,500-5,000 people crowded into small one or two storey homes made of plywood, corrugated iron, cardboard, and sheet metal, then furnished with items retrieved from neighbouring dumps. These homes pile on top of each other and have been built without any regard for safety or privacy. Whatever goes on in the house next door may as well go on in the same room. Whatever goes on two or three homes down is audible.

God's presence broke through and surpassed my self-centred expectations; admitting them had made a life-altering difference. I was prepared to trust God's control rather than try to solve things on my own. The typical response for those of us who have a materialistic Western worldview is to solve all problems we perceive. We address issues face-on, fix whatever we consider to be broken, wipe the dirt from our hands, and consider it a good day's work done. We go home to our more comfortable lifestyles and feel good about ourselves.

Near the end of the chapter in Matthew 9, Jesus walked through the crowds of sick, dying, hurting, and lonely people. He did not snap his fingers and make everything better, which he had power to do. Instead, he was overcome with compassion for the people. He shared their agony. He lived with them, but he didn't just run around fixing everything, even when he could have.

As a Westerner, I am stumped by his apparent inaction. I have been raised in a culture that strives to resolve tension and solve problems. I am baffled when God doesn't act like me, even when he could simply do what makes logical sense to me. I learned that I cannot treat life as an equation that needs solved. I must accept the unacceptable. I have to live with tension. I submit to life without answers in light of a God who cares to have shared in our human experience.

It cannot mean we just sit back and do nothing. No, not that. Never that. We keep pressing forward to improve life conditions. We strive toward the abolition of Worldwide

Poverty as it oppresses the masses. It is a life we aim to live, but it never does to rush in with all the answers and no time for relationships, that is entirely overlooking Christ's purpose. Hyped and heavily scheduled action distinctly communicates that we are Westerners, but it may not share our core message of love and compassion. We appeal to a higher calling than one that merely fixes temporal problems.

It's complicated, but it is worth walking with the crowds.

After a week in Manila, I stepped out of the air-conditioned confines of Don Muang Airport and into the heat of Bangkok. Our arrival was at late night, yet the heat was that of an unsheltered tropical beach at high noon in hot July. Unfortunately, Bangkok does not have the relief of an ocean breeze sweeping between the streets.

This was my initiation to Thailand's Not Very Hot season.

The fragrant fusion of fresh-cut Jasmine, orange blossom, saffron, and burning incense, mingled mildly with the encroaching smog abducted my olfactory sense forever. I was unwittingly exposed to the aromas of Thailand; I received an experiential education and as a result my senses trigger emotions and memories without warning at the passing of a scent.

There was more to Thailand than smothering temperatures and alluring aromas; the language was a gently passionate song; the food was an explosion of tastes and smells; the people stole my heart during those first days in Thailand. Thailand was all mystery, history, and allure. The country wears a smile of gentle passion on the face of fierce nationalism, and broadly preaches a philosophy of peace wrought with the presence of spiritual calamity. The air itself was pulsing with enticing paradoxes.

Thailand was my second stop, and though it was a mere seven days, I have never managed to completely repossess my heart.

By the second week, my ears woke to the call to worship echoing from loudspeakers of elaborately tiled mosques. Immaculate and glistening, the mosques are like jewels scattered across Islamic Asia. Beautiful gardens surround these ornate domed buildings. They are the community centres, hubs of social activity, the pre-school and elementary schools, the homeless and abused women shelters. Mosques are not only places of religious worship, but each is an holistic axis of community life. The call seemed to bring peaceful unity in its melodic enchantment. It was not what I expected.

Imagine a call to worship that brings a whole city together under one God to give him glory, even while on the train, selling food in the street, walking to work, shopping, or whatever. Something like what church bells used to be, but you don't hear church bells anymore. I wonder if these echoes, like the bells of many churches, become ineffective after a while? They sing out that God is watching over us. Our days, our time, and our lives are his. No matter what we are doing at any given time, we can come into his presence. Do they carry the same meaning for every listener?

My ears encountered many emotion-filled sounds during those fifteen days in Asia: a throaty call to Muslim worship, pentatonic chimes of gamelan drums, gonging Temple bells and guttural drones of many monks, Salsa and Blues and Flamenco in

Singapore, the enveloping silence of quiet as the sun sets over the tribal hills in the north. My ears resonate with the sounds of Asia.

My head has always been filled with philosophy, art, music, and culture, all locked behind restrictive walls of Western modernism. The mathematical deductions and logical explanations to life, promoted by church-installed education systems were all I had to go on before I set foot in Asia. Asia awoke the Eastern thinker in me. I now live in the midst of this tension.

In the philosophical realm of the East, there is no need to answer the questions, if even the questions exist. Who determines the validity of the questions? When our questions are self-serving with the intent to flaunt cultural or ethnic superiority, then the questions come from a deeply wrong motivation. Many get caught bickering over the details and rules of religious life, rather than asking what we should do with God as a Person now that he has made himself known as one. We should always be about making people wonder what to do with The God Who Presents Himself As One Of Us, even though he is far greater.

But there are still people who don't even know that there is a God. They have never been told that he loves them. We have never gone to tell them because no one has cared enough to send us. Once we know this, our feverish dedication to certain questions about the details puts us to shame.

I believe that all humans intrinsically know there is a God or that at least something like a God is out there. Ecclesiastes 3:11 says that God has put eternity in the hearts of man. If there is no end and no beginning, and yet temporal things exist, somehow the God we know has caused us to inherently understand at least a vague notion of this concept of eternity. Whether or not we have it all worked out and can explain it in three easy steps is irrelevant. As humans, we can at least acknowledge that we'd all like a chance at drinking from the fountain of youth.

Wherever you travel in the world you will meet people desperate to put a face and a name to the object of their worship. Humanity knows it's own limitations and therefore seeks the higher being. We display our need to worship, and so we worship according to our worldview, with the door to our spirituality hinged on the influence of our culture. Even atheistic societies who deny the existence of an all-knowing, all-powerful God seek to deify their leaders.

The knowledge of God has been buried deep within culture, history, worldview, and somehow deep within the articles of worship we have used to substitute God's real presence. In every culture and community his presence *is* there because nature exists, and because humans are his image bearers. Often, he has not been acknowledged or recognised. It takes a fresh recognition of the presence of God to bring God's omnipresence to the surface of every being and culture. He made it that way when he left us with the privileged responsibility to carry his truth to the world.

It is a strange thing to *be* that presence when you feel so ill equipped. By just *being* present in the midst of people who never thought to ask about God's existence raises newly relevant questions. Simply raising the question is an enormous philosophical step and is a good entry into realms of Asian life. Sharing questions about origin, destiny, and purpose has power to transcend cultural barriers that might exist. Mutual respect in friendship is forged through that kind of dialogue. You learn together more about God through you *being* rather than spouting fantastic explanations to all the questions they don't have yet.

My journey to Asia brought me home empty, yet full to the brim; torn, and somehow new; disjointed, yet never more complete. These contradictions and tensions shaped me.

MANGOES AND COCKROACHES

My teeth broke through smooth thin skin, into the thick sweetness of a fruit that must have come from Eden. Amber syrup slid down the shell of the mango. The knife shoved deep into the pit made a popsicle of my fruit dessert. It might have been that I was sick of airline cuisine, or that my unsatisfied chocolate craving was getting the better of me, but this was the sweetest, juiciest mango ever. Ed and I took fifteen minutes to savour them, like two kids eating candy for the first time at Willy Wonka's.

I have never had a mango like it. Even that one gigantic sweet green mango picked straight from the tree did not come close. In all my travels, the Manila Mango stands alone. If there are mangoes in heaven, may they be imported from the Philippines.

On the opposite end of the experience spectrum, the cockroaches of Manila were also incomparable. I had never met any real live cockroaches up to this point in life, though I'd passed over their hovels in the gutters elsewhere. I was terrified they would be in my pillow, my sheets, my bath, crawling into the crevices of my luggage and sneaking into my ear while I slept. I'd heard stories.

I wrote a chapter in my journal on cockroaches. Then I prayed fiercely. I hoped that when the time came for the inevitable cockroach meeting, I would be ready. I was counting on the smash-and-dash.

The day after The Mango, I stepped over a river of urine and garbage in the front yard of Lita's home. I nearly gagged. I did my best to hold it in and keep a smile on my face. Could you imagine being invited to a new friend's home and puking in the front hall because of the stench of the neighbourhood? Not a good first impression in a budding friendship. I could hardly avoid being queasy, though.

I would like to cover up how selfish I am, but I am not a superbly well-adjusted person. I prefer the comforts of home and the cleanliness of my privileged upbringing. Love compels me to overlook my preferences, and sometimes God gives me grace not to fail too miserably in front of onlookers.

I badly wanted to blame my queasiness on jet-lag.

The twenty-seven hour journey from Toronto to Manila's Ninoy Aquino International Airport was still working its way out of my system.

This is what jet-lag feels like: I had been dragged over a pile of jagged rocks, had the skin stripped from my bones and reapplied in sun-dried pieces with my eyelids duct taped to my eyebrows after enduring a gruelling week-long sleep strike. When I emerged slightly dazed onto the humanity-infested ramp and tripped down toward the parking lot in Manila, it was no surprise that I was delirious. I also had a headache.

The two-hour drive to the bed in Quezon City, Manila, where I would have the best sleep of my life, was accompanied by a sense of awe and nausea. How is it that solid yellow and dotted white lines don't mean a thing in many cities in the world's developing nations? Perhaps drivers think of them as nothing more than the influence of modern Western street art. It is ambitious of the government to suggest organisation out there. In Manila, lanes are a suggestion seldom heeded.

Auto-weaving is an art in motion. The ability to sew a bus through dog piles of clamouring traffic at a heart-stopping speed must be a Filipino aspiration.

As Nido weaved his way through the traffic, I was close to getting sick in the back of his truck. I managed to keep it down all the way to the house where I was staying, all the way through the first introductions to the people in the house and all the way through a bath, a change of clothes and to hitting the crisp clean sheets of the bed. I don't remember much else of that first night in Manila. Maybe the nausea carried over into the next day. Maybe jet-lag was to blame.

The next day, that nausea escorted me to Lita's front step.

You think of beauty differently after you visit Lita and her mother. Her family instantly make you one of them. That kind of beauty is unfading. Gold and diamonds can't compare.

There are tourist areas in the Philippines that I highly recommend to people looking for an aesthetically beautiful holiday. I've seen pictures. My only experience in the Philippines was more beautiful than a visit to any well-manicured resort. The squatter villages of Manila, bordered by the city dumping grounds, was my destination. I asked to go there. I was intrigued by the stories of powerful eternal differences being made in the lives of people normally subjected to impoverished circumstances.

I wanted to see people overcoming a failed environment with the love of God.

I paint a terrible picture of the community I visited, but these are the facts. The community has been constructed in the midst of the largest garbage site in Manila. I do not mean any disrespect to the people who live there. Their environment has in no way damaged their beauty, but their environment is far from beautiful.

Lita has done her best to make her home beautiful, despite it's location in the heart of one of the poorest communities in the world. Though plagued by the intrusion of poverty, threatened by pending natural disasters and terrorised by political extremists, Lita's country is a gem in the waters of the Pacific.

Lita told me she wants to be a missionary in Africa one day, to spread the love of God to people she sees as more needy than she is. In the meantime, she cares for the children in her street and brings hope where hope seems dead. She encourages her friends to look for jobs and get an education. She presses on with vision through her own struggles. She lives in that place, but Lita is not a victim to the menacing clutches of Welfareville.

Lita's mother fed me a dinner of rice with milk-fish and savoury sauce. Milk-fish is kind of a national food in the Philippines. It falls apart in your mouth and tastes like warm butter. I had to be careful not to choke on any of the gazillion tiny bones.

When they served me the fish, they all took seats to watch me eat. I think they invited neighbours over, too. I took the first bite and realised no one else was eating. I couldn't eat if they weren't eating. What if my fish was all they had? I had to insist they eat with me. I eat to share, and you can't share alone.

I didn't want any of my new friends to think I came to look at a human zoo. I wanted to do whatever it took to cross the *puti* barrier (this is a Tagalog term used to refer to Caucasian foreigners). It isn't a fair barrier for either participant and it only creates racism and alienation, as most stereotypes do. I believe in equality, not as a cultural perspective or some lofty new Western aspiration, but as part of a biblical calling. Unity should be pursued amongst brothers and sisters in Christ everywhere. You can't be unified if you are the only one eating milk-fish while everyone else watches.

We all ate together, then Lita took me for street ice cream.

We ambled single file through the street. The street is a foot-wide cracked dirt pathway meandering between a garbage filled trench and cramped houses. It leads deeper into the acrid interior of Welfareville, interrupted by slabs of broken concrete and the overflowing trench, until it is pressed tightly between shacks and sheltered from the sun by sheets of metal, stacked cardboard and torn linens. The depths of the internal core are dimly lit by a haunting green buzz and populated by weary faces.

In the belly of this beast hide the drunken, purposeless men afflicted by a vicious cycle of unemployment. Determined women, beaten down by husband, poverty, and physical labour, fear the pending inevitability of bringing another child into this forsaken corner of the world.

The women are the prevailing backbone of this struggling impoverished society. They have been beaten down, but they have not been destroyed. They hang clothes and carry buckets of water on their heads. They hum as they scrape their knuckles over a minuscule slice of soap and a household of laundry. Their eyes catch mine, despairingly lifeless for a second, but it is enough for me to seize a glimpse of their true anguish. Then, as with everywhere in this place and with these people, they are smiling, dark eyes dancing with laughter, creased at the edges, gleaming at some secret humour.

I discovered later that they smiled because of my visit. My presence reminds them that they are not forgotten. It gives them hope that the world will remember their existence if a visitor will share their story.

We bought handmade ice cream from a vendor. He took two clumps from his wobbly portable cooler atop his tricycle and wrapped them in bits of recycled paper. Lita began to tell me the story of her people. I listened as I tried to trap the dripping pineapple cream with my tongue, but it melted all over my hands.

Their story is not one of total despair. They do not want to run from their communities to some greener, better life on the other side of whatever, though I wouldn't blame them if they did. The way they see it, they have a great opportunity right in their own community. They are willing to fight for improvement and a greener living right where they are.

It all began with a single drop of water.

Water is an essential part of our existence, yet, there are so many places in the world where water is rare. It is not taken for granted because there is so little of it to be found. Welfareville was like that until the Jordan Project came along.

The Jordan Project, in partnership with the Canadian International Development Agency (CIDA), installed four water pumps in Welfareville and entrusted the distribution of the water to families within the communities. The water goes for about three pesos per gallon, a ridiculously affordable price. The intention was not only to supply fresh water; they have also made a long-term investment by using the profits from each facility to send over three hundred students to college. The students majored in Education, Philosophy, Psychology, and Engineering, among other things. Since graduation, several of the students decided to invest in Welfareville, and have been teaching at a preschool facility and providing counselling services at a youth centre. They promote family values by example; they have created a sense of belonging and hope.

The living water of Christ has brought restoration to broken people. Dedicated women lead the young people to live radically different lives than their predecessors and peers. Young men stand up against idleness and self-gratifying behaviour. They give their lives to make a real difference. They have implemented community basketball leagues to promote values and respect.

Basketball is the national sport of the Philippines. That wasn't immediately obvious to me, but it's true. A seventeen year old biology student told me how good he was at the game and explained how he is especially suited for it because of his height. Since he was sitting down, I asked him: So, how tall are you? I had to bite my tongue when he answered: Oh, very tall. I am five foot seven.

Basketball and Preschool Education are two of the avenues that these young people employ to bring life to their community.

Wanting to hear his words, the crowds pressed Jesus on every side, he pointed out their undisclosed hunger and sought to meet that basic need. When the sick came to him, he gave them eternal life because of their faith, then sent them leaping and dancing and fully healed on their way. We cannot bring healing to any society by words alone. In Welfareville, I saw action behind Christ's command to love one another.

When dark came over the city, a purple-grey quilt of stifling humidity, I was shown to the guest room. The guest room was the entire second floor: four tight walls of chipped concrete slabs held together under a flimsy tin roof. A lidless porcelain toilet sat in the corner beside a covered bucket of lukewarm water. A rusty cot lined the opposite wall, its plastic mattress thin and tattered.

I took a deep breath and set down my small pack. I was nearly eye to eye with the six inch gap between the top of the concrete wall and the angled metal roof. As soon as I had readied myself for a night of fighting for sleep, a two-inch mahogany brown cockroach slipped professionally out of a crack in the wall like a practiced magician. He stared me down, flinching briefly in an otherwise statuesque pose. I stared back, unwilling to break my gaze for fear that he'd make a beeline for my blanket.

In a way, he seemed poised as a guard for the night, attentive at his post, uninterested in me or my bed, but unlikely to turn and leave, either. I slipped into my blanket cocoon, eyes never leaving my silent foe, and tucked the edges close to my chin. I left the light on, not daring to cut the buzzing green glow to black.

My fear of a power outage mounted. Sotted shrieks from streets below soon drowned out the drone of the energy-saving bulb. I settled into a state of deliberate, solid inactivity, mentally battling visions of irrational fear.

After four jittery hours of attempted rest, the blood in my head was thumping time to rhythms of bootleg karaoke and echoing with the screams you would expect to hear in the witching hours of a slum-dog haven. My eyes scraped against the sockets, a fresh burn tearing over brittle corneas. I blinked fiercely, but no tears came. My little enemy was gone. I must have let my eyes close at the encroaching light of dawn and he'd slipped away, having scuttled across the bubbling linoleum to his crack in the wall. At least, that was where I had hoped he had gone.

A sudden, paralysed attack gripped my muscles. What if he hadn't fled to the cement? What if he'd cozied up with me for the night? What if he'd found some way to wiggle his way into my insulated covers? I willed every tip of nerve to reach out with a sixth sense, searching blindly between my sheets for any unwanted visitors. I worked up the courage to escape my cocoon, dropping bare feet to the cool floor and shaking out the blanket frantically. Nothing. I breathed, finally hauling in stale air.

It was hot. Rather than the refreshing scent of dew and the breeze of sunrise, the early morning air carried the stench of sleepy bodies and rotten fruit. I could hardly believe that the touch of clean water and crisp sheets had graced my skin only yesterday. Time had dragged itself to an agonising halt since then.

I scoured the room with red-rimmed eyes, hunting for evidence of my disappeared companion, but the light of day was blazing in through slats in the wall and rough lacerations of the fissured roof. He was gone for now, returned to his domain of darkness below the streets as the sun sent long steamy shadows across the waking city.

I bathed frugally, dipping with conservative caution into the small basin of water. I let the drops trickle across my skin, and smeared sweat and clean together before patting dry with a hand towel. There wasn't enough water to use soap. It would have to do until I got back to Quezon City.

I said goodbye and returned to Quezon City on foot, and by sidecar, bus, and jeepney.

Jeepneys overpopulate Manila and are a distinguishable late-20th Century addition. Following the American occupation of the Philippines, many army jeeps were abandoned. Locals helped themselves to these leftovers and added their own smattering of personalised gaudy creativity. These days, jeepneys are public transportation. Painted a thousand bright colours; smacked with stickers, signs, and foreign licence plates; draped in flashing Christmas lights and tinsel; multi-sized Mary and Jesus figurines affixed firmly to the hood and dashboard; leis, CDs, flags, and rosaries dangling from the rear-view mirror; these vehicles are kitsch on wheels. Jeepneys generally run two benches for about twelve passengers in the back, with the driver and three or four up front, and potentially five or six people hanging off the edges. The roof is always piled high with boxes, cartons, luggage, and sometimes more people. There's always room for one more.

That day, the one more was a quiet rooster, graciously offered to me by his owner, just in case I was absolutely dying to handle a rooster while feigning ease and comfort in the sweaty confines of this tawdry human toaster-oven. I winked, acknowledging his joke, and we got a laugh from our packed vehicle audience. The rooster did not seem too enthralled that I handle him, either.

I was shamefully grateful to arrive back at the house and flop down on my crisp clean sheets under the cool of the convulsing ceiling fan. Grateful because of the cleanliness and comfort and privacy and all those things I hate to need and should probably continue to hate needing. Grateful because who knew that two hours of travelling could be so tiring in comparison to twenty-seven hour international jet-lag? Grateful because I did not have to live in Welfareville. It was for that particular gratefulness that I was ashamed.

I think I will carry a bit of that shame with me wherever I go. It is somehow shameful that I was born a *puti* into North American society with only one sister. I received an education beyond that which many people will ever dream or imagine. I can enjoy comforts that my friends in the two-thirds world will never know. It is inherently shameful, and we who are like this should rightfully be ashamed, not of our Good Fortune as so many would like to attribute, nor of our hard-work-that-got-us-here as others may assert, but simply because we were born into this, and Lita was born into that. It's okay to be sorry, it's okay to be ashamed, but we, like her, cannot wallow there. We must recognise the privilege of our position. We have to live according to the much we have been given, for the sake of our brothers and sisters.

I believe that we are afraid to live like Mother Theresa because we think we might lose something. Jesus said that whoever gives up life for his sake will ultimately gain it, and he promised a more abundant life as a result. There is more dignity in that than anything money or earthly status can buy.

We are radicals because we follow Christ. We imitate the way he lived. Radical living requires something wholly other than putting ten percent in the plate and feeling sorry for poor people on the other side of the world. When we know them as brothers and sisters our actions in love make the difference. When we stop chasing after earthly satisfaction, we will be truly satisfied. Our enjoyment of God will be expressed in our lives as we are poured out for the sake of his kingdom. There is no better pursuit.

Dengue Drip: Part I

I have no idea how to insert an IV. I never thought I would need to know. My severe lack of medical knowledge doesn't come as a surprise to anyone who knows me well enough. I'm no candidate for the medical profession. I get faint at the sight of blood and needles. I've heard if you put an IV in wrong you can put a person into septic shock. The thought alone makes me queasy.

As I packed my bags for the fourth time that year, I didn't once think about putting in an IV. It wasn't on my need-to-know list. I was more interested in figuring out how many pairs of underwear I could live with for twelve weeks. I usually get it all into a bag small enough to take as a carry on. If I could vacuum pack it, I would. I take the important travel items: minimal clothing, my music, a novel, something to write in, a pocket bible.

We boarded a plane at 10pm with the mediocre dark of summer shrouding Toronto. Among the members of our small group were my good friends Alicia and Melissa. We already had joint overseas adventures under our belt, so we were ready for this, though I could sense a touch of nervous anticipation in our midst about the unknown.

On the flight, I memorised the city map of Luang Prabang in my travel guide to Laos. It's a small city in the north of Laos, heavily frequented by tourists, populated by the gentle Lao, a variety of tribal peoples, and a hundred or more pagodas and temples. We would stay there for a few nights, but I was looking forward to the smaller towns and villages along the way, the places we'd have to get to on foot, small motorised boat or dirt bike. Those places were not listed in my guide book.

As the flight began its descent into Los Angeles, I closed the book. The undying lights of the expansive city below struggled to shine beneath a sheath of midnight smog. Los Angeles is a world away from small northern towns along the Mekong River, but a few local memories crept into my mind as I braced gently for landing.

I learned highway driving in Los Angeles. For my first experience on a highway I crossed Los Angeles in a borrowed car. I picked up a friend in Pasadena and we drove the I-15 down to Tijuana, Mexico. We crossed the border on foot; the traffic lines for the crossing stretched days long. After a few hours in town, shopping, eating, talking, fending off men armed with tequila bottles and spouts, we headed back north. This time, we took the scenic I-5 along the coast. It was an amazing drive. We stopped at several beaches along the way, from sunset until the wee hours of morning.

My memories of Mexico and Southern California faded as the flight touched the tarmac at LAX, the lights of the runway bringing me back to earth with the plane. I would not stop here for more than a couple of hours before heading across the Pacific.

I wish I could say I slept most of that series of flights, but I didn't. I tried. It wasn't my first trip to Asia, but I hadn't been to Laos yet. I was excited. The others with me were depending on me to feed them, get them a place to sleep every night, and generally have a great experience. No pressure. So, maybe it was a combination of excitement and nervous anticipation that kept me reluctantly alert.

When we finally arrived in Chiang Mai some twenty hours later, we were exhausted. While the team slept, I worked. I checked my email and pored over a few maps, studying each step of our anticipated journey. To clear my head, I went out with some local friends for a bite to eat, and finally slept the night through.

The next morning we had a late rise and appreciated an orientation session to familiarise us with some of the local customs where we'd be heading. After a few cups of coffee, we took a bus to the border town of Chiang Khong. It was four o'clock in the afternoon by the time we arrived. We needed to stretch and walk. Our bodies were already sensing the abuse of being folded into awkward positions and we still had a long journey ahead.

We found a place to stay for the night. I'm not sure it was intended to be a hotel, but the one room house had three beds and we gladly accepted. It was just big enough for the four of us to stretch out our constricted bodies. The house sat on the Thai side of the river-border. We would be at the crossing first thing in the morning.

We bought drinkable water, bread and instant coffee for tomorrow's breakfast, and ate dinner before tucking in for the night. The low-set window in the room lay wide-open and I was less concerned about thieves than the dengue that lurked in the humid shadows of the jungle. A flawless mosquito net was essential.

I do not take malaria prophylaxis when I travel. I figure, if you're going to get malaria, you should get to a hospital within a day or two for treatment at the first flu-like symptoms. I'll take that risk over the severe psychological side effects that come packed into every bottle of quinine. Dengue, however, is something I have become very cautious about, especially in Asia. There is no vaccine, no prophylaxis, no cure. You just get it (if you're unfortunate) and wait it out, and hope it's not one of the really bad strains.

I knew a guy who contracted a particularly evil strain of dengue while working in Cambodia. After his third time with the illness, he left for a while, fifty pounds lighter and psychologically beaten down. I remember talking with him shortly after his release from hospital. He told me he asked God to take his life from him so that the pain would end.

I made sure our nets were free of defect.

We tucked our nets in tightly for a short night sleep. We'd be at the river-border crossing by six in the morning.

*****

By first light we were on the rickety dock; backpacks in tow, passports in hand, coffee in veins. We crossed on a well-used water vehicle somewhat better than an oversized raft. The Lao border was not crowded. A few other tourists had the same idea as we did and joined us in the immigration line, single file along the wooden dock to the service window of a small cement block at the edge of the pier.

Generally, what backpackers do is keep an eye out for someone who looks like they know what they're doing, then stick to them like Velcro. I was already changing our money from Thai Baht in a slim wallet to Lao Kip in an oversized ziploc bag (inflation is a beast) by the time I realised our travel-savvy Velcro was in full use. A couple of girls were following our lead at the money exchange. They followed us to the Mekong River boat and eventually tag-teamed all the way to Luang Prabang.

Our river transportation was three metres long and a metre wide. Four people could sit comfortably with bags and a driver. In Laos, it was good for twelve people, doubled up, squished into the hull with legs tucked up tightly in front, backpacks squeezed between bent knees. We collectively found this an extremely difficult way to travel, especially our full-figured new Israeli friends. The other option was by road, but that would take twice as long as ripping down the Mekong River in a jam-packed 120 horse-power canoe. They opted to join us on the water after weighing the options.

Three hours into the trip, we slowed from the ripping clip to a gentle pace. The boat stopped at a restaurant on a dock. The driver cut the engine and the captain signed that we should get out for something to eat. Our group of twelve unfolded limbs from cramped positions, assisted one another to the dock, stretched, ached, groaned, laughed at ourselves, and gained our land-feet again. We climbed a set of ramshackle steps to a shaded picnic table area over the water for a bite of the local fare.

It was nearing noon. The scorching sun was high in the sky. A dank humidity had set in, but we were momentarily relieved to have the whipping warm wind off our faces.

The ragged group was an eclectic sort, thrown together by chance of travel. Despite our journey thus far, most of the twelve were smiling. The Australians promptly got to work on clearing the house of Lao Beer as though it was their sole responsibility. They were very efficient. A young American couple, dressed too perfectly for adventure travel, set themselves apart from the group. I got the feeling there was some dissension in those ranks. Our Israeli friends made a fast break for the bathroom.

Still cramping, our group of four found a table with a menu and a pitcher of clean water. The menu came full of pictures and we ordered veggies, noodles, and something that looked like chicken. We ate plenty to keep going and just as we were about to head back to the boat, I stopped in at the bathroom.

I'm not one to shy away from potty talk. When you travel to some of the places I've been, it comes up from time to time. The toilet at this place was porcelain ivory, which was nice, in comparison to some toilets I've met in less exotic locations. It was closed in by a shaky sunburnt shed hanging precariously over the water, broad slats in the siding, and floor boards that creaked fearsomely, but it was a porcelain toilet bowl at least.

In the shed, there was enough room for half a person.

When I pulled the chain to empty the contents (water not included), I looked straight through the hole in the floor under the bowl, straight through to the muddy waters sluicing along below.

I made a quick mental note:

Do not swim in the Mekong River.

Do not allow any of the other twelve (six of whom were currently well on their way to after-lunch-drunk) tip that canoe.

We redressed our exposed skin with long sleeves, bandannas, and hats, despite the scorching humid heat, and assumed our cramped positions in the tiny boat among our travel companions.

The jungle that looms up on either side of the russet river is alive with wild sounds: shrieking monkeys, exotic birds, savage dogs and squirrels, and other rodents. We heard zilch of this from our hemi-motored canoe as it whipped along the water.

Our driver, well equipped with raven-black motorcycle helmet and gloves, silent, serious, and able to take our small boat around the curves of swift currents at frightening speeds, made me wonder if *The Stig* might be Lao.

There were a couple of things I thought about before I fell into a half-waking trance in a completely upright position, face bared to the gale-force wind:

1. I could probably get up on a slalom ski behind this canoe.
2. I hope we have enough gasoline to get to the city. There are too many of us crammed in here, and he's burning fuel awfully fast.

I nodded off somewhere between frightening visions in my overactive imagination: a broken up boat, paddling through poo-brown water in heart-stopping panic to slippery shores, being stranded along the feral banks of the river, sharing meals of monkey brains and fire-charred squirrel-rat with The Lao *Stig*, one set of very unhappy newlyweds, two obviously non-Mossad-trained Israelis, and a loudly large group of well-liquored Aussies ...

*****

Less than three hours after lunch, we arrived in Luang Prabang. We were a wind-blown, sunburnt, partially disintegrated bunch of bent out of shape misfits, ready to embark on the adventure of finding food and shelter for the night.

Our Israeli friends clamoured behind us up the steep muddy hill to the song-tows gathered near the road that would take us to the small city. We bartered our way to reasonable transportation and the six of us hoisted our bags and bodies into the back of the song-tow and sat along the facing benches.

Our group of four had left most of our stuff in Chiang Mai with friends and were travelling with very small overnight packs. Not so for our kitchen-sink-hauling friends. Inspired by our lightweight travel, they were already discussing what they could get rid of and live without for the duration of their trip.

The vehicle crawled up the incline to the main road and puttered toward the centre of the small city along roughly paved roads. Three minutes into the journey, the song-tow busted a flat. The song-tow driver got out and told us we were too big. I'm not kidding. His words. He slid a strapless spinal board from behind one of the benches to lay on, pulled a tire out (of his back pocket?) and told us he'd be twenty minutes.

We waited.

It was hot and sticky. I could hear the darkest spots on the pavement sizzling. We stood in the abusive sun and waited.

Twenty minutes passed a couple of times. We contemplated alternate transportation, such as feet. In the midst of a discussion on how far a walk it might be to the city centre, the driver announced that the spare tire was ready to go. Another twenty minutes in the back of the lopsided song-tow brought us to the heart of Luang Prabang.

We wandered into a massive double-doored hotel, tight behind a sweaty mob of tourists. The place was hopping with foreigners and the rank odour of armpits and bhanged-up ciggies. Our small group unanimously vetoed the hotel without discussion. We didn't come to Laos to sit around swapping trail-tales and tokes. Our Israeli friends, however, snagged the last room available and apologised about ditching us. We wished them a good journey and headed out to the streets for a walk. We needed to find something less stereotypical, preferably something that didn't smell like a chain-smoking skunk.

Joey was out doing his best to advertise for his hostel, to find tenants for the night or longer. He got our attention, so we swung by to check the place out. He and his family had turned their skinny four-storey apartment into a three room hostel, complete with communal bathroom. It would do. It was five bucks a night for the room. There was a double mattress and a twin mattress side by side on the concrete floor with room for our packs. A tall window gave us a view of the dirt street below.

We each took three minute turns in the water-box spraying lukewarm water around us with a dash of soap. For a couple hours, until the heat of day died down, we crashed on the mattresses to nap or read. I wrote in my journal. Downstairs, after a rest, we made conversation with Joey and friends, and even learned some essential phrases in Lao.

By early evening, we had managed to pull some presentable clothes from the depths of our shallow packs. We went in search of an authentically Lao dinner.

On recommendation from Joey, we found an old French-style house that had been converted into a restaurant. It was a quiet, candlelit estate. Lush green gardens surrounded the two-storey cement-block house. They found us a table on the balcony overlooking the gardens.

We were served a rendition of The King's Meal: papaya salad, sticky rice, roasted chicken, spicy beef strips, steamed rice, unrecognisable veggies, and ornately carved fruit. They delivered an artistic display of desserts and topped the experience off with some real (not instant) coffee.

By the time we returned to our room at Joey's house, we were well-fed and exhausted. We slept cramped, but gratefully cooled to the rhythm of the ceiling fan.

*****

We spent four days in the city. We gathered stories of people's experiences, walked many kilometres, climbed a thousand steps and prayed in circles for hours at the city's hilltop pagodas.

We talked with children, tailors, shopkeepers, monks, and wanderers. We sweat through everything and shed pounds of cellulite. The heat sucked our energy dry and tangled with our short tempers. The sun taunted our pale skin beneath sweat mingled sunscreen and sticky mosquito repellent. We craved cool baths every few hours.

The Lao bathe wrapped in sihn (a traditional Lao skirt), splashing themselves with water from buckets. Barely sheltered from the public, make-shift showers can be found in unguarded corridors, on rooftops, or in alleyways between the houses. Privacy is rare among people living in such close quarters.

We pressed on through the heat, wishing for a shower. The scent and suds of fresh jasmine soap filled the streets to tempt us as we walked.

We learned the Lao term for what it means to be very tiny: noy.

Noy was also the name of a young girl we met. She was ten, maybe eleven at the time. She chased us around the market, throwing deals at us and attempting to tantalise us with her fantastic offers of inexpensive cloth and other things we just couldn't leave the country without.

Though small, Noy was loud. Her broken English rose above the din of the packed-out marketplace. She brought us to meet her pregnant little mother and a chubby baby sister. They were stationed at a raised bamboo platform stall on one end of the colourful tarp-covered market. Tourists were Noy's bread and butter, and she certainly knew how to use that butter.

We made a halting attempt at communication for nearly an hour with her mother and the other women in neighbouring stalls. We took pictures with the baby and freely spent all our lunch money on handmade purses, skirts, and blouses. We parted ways, full of experience, empty stomachs in tow.

The streets were wet by the time we left the market. It hadn't rained, but the side roads were covered in dark splotches; it was a community responsibility to keep the dust down. Women sloshed buckets of dirty morning laundry water and greasy dish water from their front steps and doorways, careful not to smack people with a dousing as they passed by on foot or scooter. We had to take heed not to step in the way.

The pavement on the main streets, however, was dry, cracked and sizzling in the heat of the midday sun. I could feel the steam rising through my shoes, a slithering hot moisture crawling up my legs.

Dark clouds began gathering from the North. The anticipation of relief was thick in the torrid atmosphere. We retreated from the frying pan to a coffee house for a caffeine kick just before the rains hit like a cataract.

Clouds swept in and wrapped the city in a refreshing shield from the vicious sun. Thick cool drops catapulted from the sky. We finished our iced-coffee and relished a skip through the muddy rain.

We weren't the only ones. The streets had suddenly been stripped of the veneer of serious, tired, angry, confused, and frustrated travellers to laughing, jumping, dancing, rain-soaked, and giddy children, adults included. Only a few grumpy people struggled toward shelter, hands, newspapers, or backpacks doing a thin job of protecting their heads.

The pounding rain was a kindness at the end of the afternoon sun's torture. We drank it, mouths wide, licking the fat drops from our cheeks and chins. We didn't think about the probability that we had splashes of brown-tinged Mekong running down the backs of our throats. We didn't care. Conquering heat drives you to make impulsive decisions. You can't regret the adventure of impulse.

I forgot about the toilet-shed until much later.

The taste of ozone on silky lips and the scent of drenched pavement ushered us back to Joey's house, a clean shower, and fresh dry clothes.

By early morning, we would set out along the river again. This time we would head to a little town populated mostly by rice, and two distinct groups of tribal people.

*****

The welcome committee was a thin sun-scorched man in his mid-twenties with a limited grasp on English. As soon as we had disembarked, the boat driver sped away, leaving us to fend for ourselves. The town seemed deserted apart from the smiling man. His agility in plastic sandals was admirable. I doused a twinge of jealousy as I stumbled up the slope in my hiking shoes. We held our breath. I think we hoped it might prevent us from slipping backward into the Mekong.

Where you from?

He made light conversation while we struggled to maintain a foothold.

Canada.

We reached the road at the top of the riverbank. It was too early to be fighting the elements already. I needed a coffee.

Oh, Canada!

He smiled even broader and raised his eyebrows. He nodded knowingly and gave me a wink. I wasn't sure how to take that. I looked up and down the quiet dirt road and chose a direction. We headed up the abandoned street in hopes of finding somewhere to stay, maybe something to eat, and some coffee. The young man kept pace and kept talking.

Smoke ganja?

It was more of a suggestion or an offer, not a conversation piece. His knowing look suddenly registered. I wondered, was it the Canadian thing or was it just something they ask every tourist that shows up? It was my turn to raise my eyebrows at him.

Coffee.

I said the word clearly to avoid confusion with any other drug. The thought of morning java with a wad of weed had never crossed my mind, but this one-road-town was so dead they were desperate for public. Most boats gave it a miss on their way to more appealing stopovers.

The Ganja Salesman shifted his offer to bootleg VCDs and a couple hours at a local Karaoke Bar. I forced a smile. Coffee and Accommodation were our priorities. He shrugged and pointed toward the top of the road. Then he left us to fend for ourselves.

We shuffled along toward the end of town.

At the top of this brush stroke of bare civilisation stood a sturdy, spacious and completely desolate house. I looked over my shoulder to see if our welcome party was still in sight. Suddenly, losing my mind was creeping up the list of viable options for handling the realities of our pending stay.

The house was built entirely of teak, bathed in jasmine and the scent of freshly cut wood. It was the only hotel in town. It was the sole restaurant. It was the height of all tourist attractions in the village. It gave the impression of being one hundred percent unoccupied.

It took a lingering few minutes for our hosts to realise they had guests, but a sleepy-eyed teenager finally appeared from behind a bamboo curtain pulling a shirt over his dishevelled head. We booked in as the exclusive guests of the establishment and were offered a river-view table for lunch.

The house juts out from the side of a banked hill overlooking the waters below. Our low table lounged beside a short railing, metres above the rushing Mekong. Multicoloured Buddhist prayer flags, clunky bells of dried gourd skins and coconut shells, and freshly cut strings of jasmine dyed in the colours of the Lao flag lined the overhanging thatch roof.

A bright eyed young girl in a Pokemon T-shirt and mismatched sinh showed up with a menu. She bowed and offered me the menu with two hands. I accepted, repeating her mannerisms. The menu was entirely in Lao: no translation, not one picture of food.

I took a deep breath and pointed to a few long lines of Lao script. The young girl nodded and smiled, but didn't write anything down. I should have learned the words for chicken and rice before crossing the border. I said a silent prayer that we would get something recognisable. Where was the English-speaking Ganja Salesman when you needed him?

I remembered the word for water: *noa.* I ordered some and used my limited skills in *Charades* to explain that we intended on drinking the *noa* lest she think we needed a bath. Given our ratty state, she might have been confused. She hummed, smiled, bowed, collected the menu, and disappeared behind a closed door at the other end of the room for three hours.

We settled into our very comfortable chairs and waited.

I had forgotten to order coffee.

An hour into our wait, I began to wonder about my aptitude in international communication. We convinced ourselves that they probably had to putter up river to get water or hit the early morning market for a live chicken. The town had been fairly silent when we arrived.

Two other young girls suddenly emerged. They catered to our entertainment needs by blasting Karaoke through a set of mammoth speakers. Dancing Lao script accompanied low-budget videos on a screen against the wall. We were invited to take up the microphone and sing along. Maybe they mistakenly assumed we could read Lao because of my stunning expertise with the menu.

We refused the mic politely, which provoked a programme change for *The Macarena* on repeat. We pretended not to know that song either. Gradually, the wavering high toned vocals, electric drums, bells, and flute sounds of Lao pop music screeched over the Mekong. It killed peace, wildlife, and our conversation.

Three hours later, a few small plates of cooked meat and vegetables were delivered to the table with a pitcher of drinking water and four glasses. It was barely enough to take the edge off our hunger, but we were grateful. We ate slowly and carefully, taking our time with each bite to make it last.

The midday sun was high in the sky by the time we finished eating. We paid our bill and went for an afternoon walk.

It was a stupid decision, really. The sun was remorseless. It was a grimy stroll through town. Our clothes were wet, clinging to our skin, but we pressed on, determined to see and learn and pray. We split up to cover more ground, to be less daunting with our foreign presence. We held onto a slim hope for meaningful interaction.

I visited a small monastery on the other side of town. The few monks in residence had just finished hand-washing their robes. A lopsided row of saffron and sangria linen stretched across the balconies. Wafts of jasmine, sandalwood and the fragrant champa flower sifted over the walls to the street. The wooden gate to the property sat a few paces down a brief dip from the road. It was well painted, though thin, hinged between two whitewashed cement block posts. The door was wide open and welcoming, but I didn't enter.

Inside, champa shrubs filled the gardens; broad green leaves fanning out from the small but sturdy, pale, golden five-petalled national flower. White jasmine extended along the interior, spilling over the walls to adorn the street. The blend of aromas was intoxicating in the oppressive heat of the afternoon. The scent would trick any visitor into believing there was a lush palace of resplendent gardens behind the walls, but it was a simple teakwood residence.

I stood at the cement pillar at the gates and a pile of dust on the side of the road. It was easy to ignore the dirt, sweat, and the scorching sun behind me while wrapped in the shade and scents of such a peaceful garden.

In a place where the only representation of foreigners was encapsulated in that telling question, "Smoke ganja?" it was difficult to imagine ever being seen as an agent of truth, an ambassador of peace, someone who carried a selfless message of hope. Most foreigners were viewed by these locals as having a selfish ambition to rip through culture and trample tradition in an indulgent, hedonistic, drunken tour of Southeast Asia.

From itching scalp to dust-caked toe I became overwhelmed with the mass of the task, the millions affected, and the impossibility of it all. How can you call people to remember an origin from which they have been severed effectively for millennia? How can you embrace culture and tradition without first being able to read a menu?

I breathed in deeply. The freshness of life and beauty surrounded me in the flowers. The touch of love was evident in their entwining embrace. The truth of their existence cooled my flesh and spoke to my spirit.

A smile broke my cracked lips. The subtle voice of nature whispered everywhere around me about the truth and love of the Creator. If people stop to listen, they will hear nature breathe. It speaks of goodness and perfection. It tells the story of brokenness. It reveals holiness and order, forgiveness and freedom. I prayed that the monks at this monastery would listen intently.

I had a staggering conversation with my Creator by those doors that afternoon. I walked away assured of the power in the voice of his creation, though still moved by the daunting task.

By the time I arrived at the house, the bole brown river had blackened beneath the copper light of the setting sun. It slunk eerily past town, shrouded by unkempt jungle overhang. The monkeys had started screeching as the dusk settled into night. I'd like to think of monkeys as musical, in a Bon Scott sort of way.

We hunkered down on wooden platforms, weakly shielded by flimsy mosquito nets from all kinds of living things. A couple of nasty rats came venturing for morsels in our backpacks by the light of the Mekong moon. The mosquito nets were almost not good enough to prevent them from cuddling up for the night.

Amid the bats, rats, mosquitoes, snakes, screeching monkeys, and cawing of exotic birds, we flinched in and out of sleep for a little more than five hours. I don't think it is a stretch to say that it was the worst night of Alicia's life. It was like trying to sleep peacefully to AC/DC's *Thunderstruck* on Surround Sound.

By sunrise, the monkeys had decided to cool the chaos. We were ready for daylight, coffee, a dose of Valium and the road to Chiang Mai.

We left town that afternoon. The burden on my heart had increased, but I was assured that nature's war for the soul will continue until eternity is discovered. The jungle resonates terror by night while the rocks cry out about the glory of God.

Whatever the rocks don't say, the flowers will whisper in the cool of the day.

*****

The journey back to Chiang Mai was badly rained on. Our boat arrived very late to the border. We crossed despite sheets of torrential rains and promptly discovered that all public transportation routes back to the city had closed for the day. As in most tropical countries, everything was cancelled due to the severe rains.

We were stuck. The rest of the people on our boat went to find somewhere to stay for the night. It was only four o'clock in the afternoon, and we had plenty of time to get back to the city.

My group huddled for shelter under a makeshift shed. I used my limited Thai to convince a guy with a truck that he needed to take us to Chiang Mai for a little more than gas money. He was not eager to assist me in our dilemma, so I begged and pleaded, and added a few more baht to the deal, until he said, Okay, and jumped up from his spot. He made a quick dash through the rain for the cab of his pickup truck. I signalled for my crew to fall in before he left without us in his sudden urgency.

It was a double cab. We barely fit.

I sat between our driver and his young companion. I clutched the dashboard, the seat, my knees, and whatever else I could grasp as he ripped along winding mountain roads at a hundred and forty kilometres an hour. I realised about an hour into our journey that he probably wanted to make the return trip before nightfall.

In the north part of Thailand, towns line the road. Houses press dangerously close to the pavement. Rural children are not careful about watching for speeding traffic in front of their houses. They dashed out into the street without warning. I tried to encourage the anxious driver to slow his roll. He smiled, eased up for a second, then squeezed his foot to the floor with greater intensity. We were lucky he didn't hit any kids along the way. There were a few very close calls.

To our dismay, a mother hen and her babies could be seen crossing the road up ahead. The driver pressed a hand to the steering wheel, the pealing horn cried out a warning, but what could anyone do? Run into the street and risk human life for a chicken? He never once eased his foot off the pedal.

The hen waddled faster, fanning her useless wings to scurry her chicks to the side of safety. The driver pulled the wheel to the right, then the left, then tried to regain control as the truck swerved slightly from the jerky movement. He sucked his teeth, hmmm'ed, lifted his foot off the gas, and then launched a tire into the air right over the poor chicken. The truck thumped against the animal as though it were taking a minor speed bump.

He floored the pedal and tried his best to ignore the heavy silence in the cab.

He played some loud awful music.

He laughed a little with his companion. He made a forced attempt to lighten the mood, but there were tears in the back seat. I felt like I should say something.

The worst part about the incident was that the chicken had likely been a source of livelihood for a family in the village. They no longer had that income. In our carelessness, we had just crashed through and robbed them of their resources.

The thought struck me that it could have been a person. I was caught speechless in contemplating that possibility. The mocking melodies of romantic ballads cranked out as we sat there in stunned silence for another half hour. The driver careened over dipping hills and around sharp bends. I urged him quietly, just one more time, please, *kah*, to slow down, *kah* (the Thai word used to make things more polite). This time, he complied with an awkward guilty smile.

We made it to the market in Chiang Mai without further incident. The sun was just starting to dip over the horizon, but the light of day would linger for another few hours. I offered to buy our driver something to eat, perhaps some rice and chicken before he left. With a cringe, I realised that nobody felt like eating chicken. He declined, itching to get back up north before it was too dark.

I can't remember what day of the week it was, but the place was packed with tourists, Thai, and a few elephants here and there. Already, the stalls of the night market were buzzing with activity.

My small group made our way back to the place we'd left the rest of our stuff. After a quick shower, we compiled a short budget update and shared reflections with our hosts. We still had enough energy to go out to the market for a bit.

Dusk had cast purple shadows among the green light of the market stalls. The mixed aroma of freshly cut jasmine, fried peanuts, lemongrass, mint and basil rose up from food stalls lining the pavement. We found our appetites, but we had suddenly become avid vegetarians.

A young elephant seemed lost in the human shuffle. Confused, his eyes darted to the people around him, searching for someone. He lifted his foot to take a cautious step, but his leg only dangled in the air, unsure of which direction he'd like to set down. The lostness overwhelmed him.

Just in that moment, when a quiet panic threatened to strike, a barefoot boy in silk Thai-style pants with a short wooden prod in one hand, devouring a custard pastry in the other, came to the rescue.

The young elephant seemed to sigh in relief. He immediately found his careful footing, his big ebony eye locked on his little companion. He padded on, reassured by the presence of the skinny shirtless youth at his side. It was a profound level of trust from a two tonne animal for such a small boy.

The elephant reminded me of how foolish I am whenever I lack trust in the God of the universe.

BURNT ...

I trusted God immensely for those first four years as a missionary. I asked God to provide and I was amazed that he did so abundantly. I told the story of that kindred soul, Hudson Taylor, to hundreds of people. I told stories about friends like Lita and Joey, the masses of desperate people like Noy and the Ganja Salesman, and many others I met along the way.

As listeners heard their stories and realised the great need that still remains in Asia, they caught a spark for the cause.

There are many people in Asia who still do not know God. They have never heard that death has no victory, that we can live free from sin and free from the looming threat of death (I Cor. 15:54-55).

Some Christians live so fluidly in material and spiritual freedoms it has become easy to forget that others do not share those same liberties. During those four years, it was in my job description to remind people of the bigger picture of God's purpose and love. I urged participation in missions and administrated the details of their involvement, and all the while, I trusted that he would meet my every need.

The message of God's love had first created a spark in my life as a child. Taylor's example ignited a fire within me for missions. The job was no longer officially my duty, but I would not stop telling the stories. The experiences were burnt into my consciousness as a permanent mark on my blazing soul.

ONE AEROPLANE RIDE AND A CONTINENTAL SHIFT TO PUBLIC CARS

I started toward home from Asia, my final trip of the year, potentially for a very long time. It seemed as though I had spent the past four years in a state of perpetual jet-lag. At the start, I had set out on a steep learning curve; as I boarded that final plane out of Asia, I felt I had only just scraped the surface.

I boarded the JAL flight, aware that a chapter in my life was coming to a close. I had my mind on the future. I was facing a decision and I had faithlessly asked God for a sign to help me make it.

Alongside the work in Asia, I had visited Latin America several times with youth and youth leaders from my church. My dream was as strong as ever: facilitation of cross-cultural educational experiences for young Canadians, to train them hands-on in mission.

I had an open invitation to live with a Dominican family and a desire to learn Spanish. Instead of moving forward, I was waiting for some kind of sign. I already knew I should go, even if I couldn't see all the connections. However, as we grown-up humans often do, I wanted more confirmation.

My flight left Narita Airport from Tokyo toward Chicago, where I'd catch a connection to Toronto. As a single passenger,

I got a middle seat. To my left was a Japanese business man who quickly completed his entry documents for the United States in rapid Japanese scrawl. He ate his meal in silence, watched a movie, and slept for most of the trip with an embroidered hand towel over his face. To my right sat a thin middle aged man who appeared to be Japanese and seemed confused about everything, including himself.

As he turned over the bilingual (Japanese-English) entry card for about the twentieth time in five minutes, my distracted brain couldn't help but wonder if he could read. I was having a difficult time understanding how a well-dressed, internationally travelling, Japanese-looking passenger might be illiterate. Illiteracy is not prominent in Japan.

I wanted to help him, but the chances that he spoke English seemed slim, and my Japanese is as good as Domo Arigato, Mister Roboto. I tried not to think about him and scraped my eyes across the text of the latest in my collection of aeroplane paperback novels.

Finally, he pulled out his passport and set it on the tray table in plain view.

I couldn't help but smile; I had assumed very wrongly about my neighbour.

Quieres ayuda? I offered to help. I looked from his Peruvian passport to his documents, and up to his staring black eyes.

Usted habla español? He nearly attacked me with happiness. I speak Spanish. A smile spread from his face to his heart, a relief that washed over him from sighing shoulders to shaking fingers. Then he laughed. What are the chances that he would be sitting beside someone who could speak Spanish? (I was not fluent. My Spanish was passable.)

He was suddenly my new best friend. I fumbled tongue-tied with my limited Spanish. We were amazingly able to complete his documents. He asked about what I was doing in Japan, which led to me haltingly explain my work, and that I was connecting from Thailand.

As I spoke, he bent over, indicated with an upraised finger that I should pause. He was looking for something in his knapsack at his feet. He pulled out a tiny, relatively unused leather-bound Bible, and opened it on his tray table. He had some questions he thought I could answer.

We spent the next three hours stumbling over language through theological concepts, what it means to have religion, and how that differs from *knowing* God in a real and personal manner, biblical application to real life situations, why dos and don'ts won't matter where love is the rule, and how such a Holy God could be also so full of love. Not your typical in-flight small talk.

He told me about how he got to Japan. He is a third generation ethnic Japanese, born and raised in Peru, and decided to get in touch with his distant and forgotten roots. He told me of the thriving, yet largely overlooked community of Spanish-speaking immigrants living in Tokyo.

During his three year visit, that sub-society became his community, which explained how he hadn't learned to read or write Japanese. As Japanese is an entirely other system of language than Spanish, it had been impossible to learn without intensive study. He had neither time nor money for intensive study. He confessed he could get by in Japanese chit-chat, but the only language he had truly mastered in life was Spanish.

We watched a movie together, talked through the random and confusing array of meals the airline served across scattered time-zones, sat in silence at intervals, and then helped each other through security, immigration, and baggage claim at the airport. He was grateful for the Spanish language signs and customs agents at O'Hare Airport. I was grateful not to have had to take that long trek alone.

We parted ways to catch connecting flights that would take us to opposite extremes of our shared hemisphere, but the meeting had brought some strange spiritual encouragement. We'd hold onto it, though not to each other. We'll meet again in an entirely other hemisphere when todays and tomorrows are over. The last glimpse I got of him was of his dark eyes creasing upward in a broad smile, a big shameless wave, and a holler across the crowded airport: *Hasta luego, hermana*.

I had been looking for a sign. God planted an opportunity in my path.

I turned in my wings with the Asian organisation and started making tentative plans to shift continents for a while. I had a personal goal of learning Spanish (I mean, fluent) and seeking open doors to bring young people into cross-cultural educational experiences. I had the green light, but still struggled with scores of unique uncertainties. Questions loomed over me about status and finances, among other insecurities.

The Sunday before I left, I received two cheques. They had been delivered to my house by people unknown to each other. The sum was about fifty cents more than the cost of the flights I had reserved for that Thursday. I don't believe in coincidences.

I arrived in the Dominican Republic and spent the first month struggling through language. I realised early the first week of my new immersed life that my halting Spanish was quite terrible. I learned how to get around on public transportation without getting severely overcharged. I searched for opportunities in local ministries in which our church youth could get involved. Then, just when I was about to throw in the towel on the whole thing because finances were running thin and did not look to be sustainable for much longer, I was asked to interview at a local Christian school. The financial input would give me just enough to continue to live by in the country.

It always makes me laugh when I think of these teetering moments of faith between pressing on and giving up based on presently (un)available finances. It confirms to me what I believe at my core about finances in ministry: Finances, while they *can* determine the potential for continuing a certain ministry, should never be the driving factor whether a certain ministry should be pursued. They can be a deciding factor, at the ultimate last moment, when the last straw of impossibility falls down on the breaking back of a camel, whether the ministry should happen in whatever way the current unmet budget suggests. We might rearrange the budget, reconsider the details, or vary certain elements of that ministry. However, readily available finances or financial security should never decide whether we can chase or work toward any ministry.

J. Hudson Taylor once said, "God's work, done in God's way, will never lack God's supply." His words have always held great weight in my life. That supply sometimes comes in the way of cold hard cash or personal cheques; other times it comes through much needed friendship and companionship, but mostly it comes clothed in the total transformation of my perspective of what support is really all about. God's supply can often shockingly have nothing to do with finances.

Over time, I had hopes for a useful building in which we could house participants and host partners. God alternately supplied even better: homes where we could stay for a time, learn culture and language, and grow spiritually alongside local families throughout the country. It was a very immersed experience with deep lasting relationships that many of the participants still maintain despite countries of distance and time zones of separation.

God did not provide a twelve-seater vehicle, either. He instead supplied us with the ever-compelling, miraculously functioning, crammed, resurrected, and adventuresome *carro publico*.

The ride in a public car is a fascinating one-time-only experience for visitors to the island. Tourists don't usually come back in droves for a second trip in a *carro publico*. This mode of public transportation is a daily necessity, and the ride is usually slimy, sweaty, stinking, and sour. If you take all that and put it aside, the reality is that the conversations you can have with people in a *carro publico* are invaluable.

Open to a variety of subjects, the generally exasperated and overheated public risk mounting these rickety shells of mid-80s Camrys and Corollas with a camaraderie that surpasses the demeanour of most baseball teams. We have a suffering in common. That alone (besides being sat on or helplessly being forced to sit on your neighbour) breaks whatever icy tension might linger in the scorching heat.

I have talked about love and politics, love and finances, love and the weather, love and baseball, love and religion, love and God, love and a society roughly lacking in its display of love for one another. Love is a big deal in Latin America.

I have prayed for and received prayer from total strangers while riding public cars. I have cried, laughed, and got red-hot politically passionate along with my public car companions. I have read scripture, challenged their faith, had my own faith challenged, received random acts of generosity and been able to bless others — just by taking the *carro publico*.

One especially difficult morning in that first year I thought I might not be able to press on. I was about to give up, I wasn't seeing ministry possibilities, and I felt very alone. A song came on the radio of the *carro publico* that gently told about how when we face a thousand difficulties and run out of strength, if we lift our hands to God we will start to feel an anointing that causes us to sing, that fills us with the fire of the Holy Spirit. When we lift our hands to God our burdens fall away and God gives us new strength to press on. The song reminded us that everything is possible when we lift our hands to him, when we praise him in whatever.

The whole car started to sing. They sang softly at first, the older woman in the back seat was the first to whisper along, but gradually the rest of us got brave and joined in. There were six passengers and the driver. We were on our way to separate jobs, represented distinct difficulties, and we didn't know each other at all, but when we started to sing together, God's Spirit filled that broken down junk heap of a car. We sat in traffic and sang together without a care. A strange thing happened: my burden was lifted, my heart was filled with comfort and my eyes with tears. I *knew* that no matter what happened, God was *already* supplying exactly what I needed.

God supplied for me in Latin America by giving me loving families who housed and cared for me as one of their own. I acquired work that helped provide for my basic needs, and which brought me into encouraging and challenging environments. I gained companionship with incredible new friends. There were enough ministry connections to see a number of young people participate in cross-cultural educational experiences that changed their lives.

It would have been a total disservice to my faith and my incarnate ministry if God had supplied me with a vehicle during that time. His supply was contrary to what I would have planned, and yet far beyond what I ever could have dreamed or imagined. Public transportation was a reminder to me of reality in my foreign home. It was often that very interaction with strangers which served to fortify my faith and remind me that I was never alone.

In the midst of common-place events, we can increase and challenge our faith. Faith presses us toward more of God, more love for others, more opportunities to speak about God's love no matter what our circumstances. That faith pushes us to see more evidence of his love and to revel in his interaction with our environment.

If we dedicate even our our concept of supplication to seeking opportunities to love people, God will provide whatever we need to do that. God shows us opportunities on aeroplanes while crossing continents or during a simple commute on public transportation. Wherever we are, God could draw near to one more person through our presence. Even if we don't get everything we thought we needed along the way.

Space to Breathe and a Borrowed Peso

I became very spatially aware when I lived in the Dominican Republic. As in many countries around the world, personal space hardly exists in much of Latin America. Most cars contain five seat belts. On the island, cars fit seven people uncomfortably, but they fit, so they squeeze. Buses cram five, sometimes six, across four spots, and though they had not been designed for it, the aisles stack standing passengers. A swaying crowd rides perilously on the steps clinging to the handle, or whatever they can find to steady their balance.

Death-by-commute is not uncommon.

Shared living spaces average the size of a standard middle class North American bedroom (though not the class associated with that space). For example, the apartment I lived in during my first years in Santo Domingo was no more than a space of about three hundred and fifty square feet, including bedroom, kitchen, a small barred-in balcony, and a waterless bathroom hemmed in by a shower curtain. There was no room for an extra door. Five of us lived there with two bunk beds. It was our running joke that we had an ocean-view property. If you shimmied up between the bars and peered over the opposing rooftops, you could catch a glimpse of the blue sea beyond.

Space was a dimension I had not previously considered a luxury. In the past, a short three-week visit had alerted me to the realities of living in considerably less space, but wedging myself into the mix on more lasting terms extracted a deep vulnerability. I had moved to the country fully aware that the living conditions alone would make me apt to expose my insecurities and ride the limits of my patience with frequency. Add the thirty degree heat and a polyester uniform, and it was a recipe for pressing any woman to her point of explosion.

Why stay? It was not necessary for me to sacrifice the comforts of everything I inherited through birth in Canada, including the luxury of space. If I made a list of perceived human hardships, the chips would stack heavily against making a life in that environment.

Fortunately, my desire to stay was not based on any level of personal comfort. It was based on my belief that if I ever wanted to help people in any way, I must first walk in at least some of their experience. It creates deeper camaraderie and fosters understanding.

I do not believe that this is a formula or a requirement for everyone, nor is it necessary in every situation. For me, because of my circumstances at the time, it was an opportunity I could not ignore.

My model is Christ in his incarnation; he showed us the lengths he would go for the love of humanity, not because he needed to, but because we would understand him better if he put on our experience. Jesus demonstrated his understanding of humanity to us by putting on our skin. He did not need to do this to understand us; he created us and understands us perfectly without the incarnation. The incarnation was for us, so that we would know his love was real. We benefit from the act. In becoming one of us he allowed us to see with our own eyes and know that he was willing to make the ultimate sacrifice. Through the incarnation, we are assured of his love and understanding.

Helping the poor is never about guilting the rich into giving up their money. That approach always seems to value the money more than the people giving and receiving the money. Equally, all the knowledge in the world about the problems of the world cannot break my heart and drive me to join passionately in another person's struggle, but a relationship with that person might. It takes time to build those relationships, and if I give of my time, I might be believed.

Money put toward long term community investments can help initiate problem solving, though it cannot be seen as the solution. Foreign experts can analyse communities and make beneficial suggestions, and this often works for a time. However, unless the people gain a vision for their own community, any solution implemented by external entities alone will be seen as an imposition of continued imperialism. That is unfortunately no solution at all.

This is not to say that we should never engage in community development work; we must continue to have heart, but we have to proceed with awareness of how we are perceived in any community we enter. We cannot be seen as community saviours; there is only one Saviour. We cannot fix what we determine needs fixing because truly, only the Holy Spirit can turn hearts.

The only worthwhile change we should pursue is one that lasts for eternity; every other change will break, crumble, or fade. Eventually, we all fade. I want to be part of something much bigger than my own short life.

We share cramped spaces and the workload. We enjoy life, and suffer ups and downs together. We learn what it means to live in someone else's shoes; they become our teachers. Reality in their experience is different than the one we come from, and though there are positive aspects and negative drawbacks in both, which we can eventually share through our relationships, we cannot strive to make their environment and experience look like ours. That can never be the goal. That still stinks of imperialism. Sometimes that means letting people take care of us, even if it seems that by some unwritten standard, they are not qualified to do so.

I learned a lot in my first year of living in the Dominican Republic. The most important thing was this: Nobody in the world needs me, my genius, my astute work ethic, or my measly pesos. They can live just fine without me coming to their rescue. They don't need me. Nobody needs me. That realisation is a fantastic philosophical starting point for any missions involvement.

The marvel of missions happens when the people in the receiving community, knowing that they don't need you, want you anyway because of who you are and not what material benefits you might have to offer. The point of missions is to form relationships that will last for eternity. Starting from the foundation of mutual relationship in equal partnership gives motivation for all kinds of worthwhile missional pursuits.

I was able to build deep, mutually trusting relationships. In those relationships, we shared dreams and goals and failures. We still strive after personal goals that remain unachieved. We reach forward together, though toward different things.

It is difficult to squash the assumptions that come with being the new girl in a Caribbean town. Local history tells people that someone like me has come to fix things, run community development programmes, set up schools, start free medical clinics, and spend time entertaining their kids. All of these are great endeavours, and while they may eventually happen, I initially came to simply share space where I was invited with eternity in mind. I came to learn.

Not every foreigner that shows up is there to achieve community development programmes. Yet, for towns across numerous developing nations, that's all the recent comparison they've got to go on, which is infinitely better than what they had a hundred years ago. History taints current perspective on an individual from any people group. It often discolours the truth, making way for stereotypes and assumptions based on race or ethnicity. Too much merit is given to stereotypes. As Christians, we should look differently at people than the world does: we have enlightened eyes that let us see a soul wrapped in the beauty of physical creation (Eph. 1:15-19).

It takes time and patient presence to work at building real friendships, based on equality and not on the usual give-and-take people have become used to in developing nations whenever foreigners enter their midst. It takes commitment, transparency, and even deliberately disappointing certain stereotypical expectations, in order to strip away the assumptions that cloud true relationships.

I cannot say that I was entirely successful at resisting the urge to help in some situations. It was impossible to keep the balance when faced with death, or the obvious hunger of another day. If I had the means to help a person asking for help, I loaned a peso. On the other hand, if I found myself empty handed along the way, I could always count on a borrowed peso.

My friend, Esperanza, usually sits at the corner of El Conde and Calle Meriño. One night, as the black slipped over the island and the moon shone bright behind rushing clouds, we sat on the curb in front of a closed up trinkety tourist shop. She talked about her long-lost daughter and reminisced about the fear of living under Trujillo. Rafael Leónidas Trujillo Molina ruled tyrannically over the Dominican Republic as Dictator from 1930 until his assassination in 1961.

Esperanza told me she thinks that someone took her daughter from her, but she can't remember when or how. I've heard her talk about this part of her life before, and some people in that part of town say she is crazy for talking like that, but I believe her.

We sat for a few minutes in silence and then she asked me to read from the Psalms. We prayed together. After a few minutes of watching people up and down the street, we ended up laughing at some of the antics of a group of loud and happy young tourists. They had turned the street into a playground in front of us. Esperanza tries to keep her sense of humour, even if they don't always let her keep her spot in the street.

When I got up to leave, I could tell she was hungry. She didn't say anything, so I asked if she had eaten at all during the day. She skirted the issue, talked about the generosity of the restaurant owners in the area, and avoided answering. She never asks me for anything. She says we're friends and she never holds her hand out to me for spare change. I couldn't leave her hungry. A full belly might help her rest more peacefully under the city's faded stars.

I left her with a toasted sandwich and a fruit juice from one of the nearby restaurants. As I approached Parque Independencia, I scrummaged around in my pockets for a few pesos, but I was going to have to borrow if I wanted to get anywhere on public transit. The meal had cost me what little I had taken with me that night. I had not planned on spending any more than transit money while I was out. I walked from Isabela la Catolica all the way to Los Heroes, thankful for healthy legs to carry me, thankful for a home, a roof over my head, a guaranteed wage, the promise of food for tomorrow, and mostly thankful that Esperanza would be well-fed, for tonight, at least.

A bus driver saw me walking, stopped his bus, and asked if I needed a ride.

No, it's okay, thanks, I don't have any bus fare with me. I confessed mid-step, sort of wary, content to walk the rest of the way, but getting tired.

Forget about it, this one's on me, it's getting dark out and I couldn't live with myself if anything happened to you.

He waved his hand, indicated that I get on his bus. It was his Dominican way of making it look like I was doing him a favour while he was helping me out. I shrugged, smiled back, and boarded the half empty bus. I was relieved not to have to walk the rest of the way.

I sat close to the front and we talked for a while about why I live in the Dominican Republic. He commented about the chances we often miss at sharing God's love with one another. By the time he left me closer to home, the conversation had been a blessing to both of us, and his act of kindness had bolstered his faith and given me a huge break, while mine had done the same for both Esperanza and I.

One act of kindness was like a waterfall of blessing along the route that night. I got home hours later than intended, and my legs were sore the next day from my 6km walk (in those shoes), but I was far more blessed in having taken the adventure and welcoming the risk than if I'd stayed at home and not bothered. It is worth seeing where your faith will take you if you give up your space to breathe and lose your pride on a borrowed peso.

When having the means to help, or the premonition to see necessary structural or societal changes could not be applied in our community, we all had to stand by together and watch death steal life in the most unfair of ways. We are only fragile humans. We all bleed red. We all eventually die. It is the one sure thing we have in common. Our search to find meaning while we still have life, so that we can explain the inevitability of death, is a search we share across continents and philosophies.

One night, when I was still living in a rural town with the Hendricks family, my urgency for communicating the truth of eternity above all other endeavours was harshly confirmed. About eight o'clock, with laughter and a full house, we had scraped something together for dinner when the doctor's cell phone rang. Sonia was on-call and the hospital was only five minutes away. Her mood turned sombre immediately. She hopped on the back of Rodney's motorcycle and they sped off to the hospital, though speed was no longer necessary.

A young girl had crossed in front of a stopped bus, had been hit by a passing jeep, and thrown fifteen feet. They put her body on the back of the nearest motorbike and raced her to the hospital, but it was too late. She had disembarked the bus only seconds previous to being swiped from the dark road, her eighteen year life jarred to an abrupt end. If she had waited for her bus to leave and crossed only when she could clearly see the headlights of approaching vehicles, she would have avoided the accident. If only.

Sonia returned within the hour, shaking her head at the senselessness of the situation. The impact had broken the girl's neck, killing her instantly. The jeep was long gone. There was no retribution. There was no bringing her back. We searched philosophically into the damp morning hours for meaning and answers. We knew *how* it had happened, we just couldn't get our heads around *why*.

Every community in the world presented with metaphysical dilemma and strives to understand. We all want to experience the feeling of understanding. We have never been convinced by simply hearing a message or reading a manual. We have been convinced when we *live through an experience*. When we listen to someone's testimony of living through experiences, it is more convincing than theories or hypotheses. The most effective way of convincing our listeners of our care and expertise in an area is to speak from our own personal experience.

José Martí, a Cuban poet, artist, and political revolutionary, said: "To know the country in the way that it works and to become one with the people in this way is the only way to see the people and the country free of it's tyrants — no matter who or what they are." Martí was instrumental in the expulsion of imperial rule in the Latin Caribbean during the nineteenth century. His philosophies guided Dominican people through thirty years of oppression under the dictatorship of Trujillo in the mid-twentieth century.

Even if you cannot agree with Marti's politics, there is something here that rings true for those of us seeking to bring hope to spiritually captive communities; we cannot be effective in bringing freedom to people's lives unless somehow, we first walk in their shoes.

During his thirty-three years on earth as one of us, Jesus did just that.

All money can do is buy material things. Worse, it will afford you the luxury of private space, so that you can separate yourself from the very people with whom you would otherwise be packed in close quarters, exposed and vulnerable, meeting the very deepest you that exists, and sharing the hope of eternity with others when there is nothing else left to share. Going there for a while is kind of like walking with Jesus and his disciples.

BURNOUT ...

In the summer of 2009, I moved from my small town life on the outskirts of San Pedro de Macoris back to the city to teach again. The apartment in Santo Domingo I moved to needed some spring cleaning. With a friend visiting from Canada, we set to work giving my room a thorough scrub down, corner to corner, ceiling to floor.

We had nearly finished and I guess I was being particular, wiping down the walls again. With a wet cloth, I swept my hand across the hastily painted cement walls, including an open electrical outlet.

We take for granted the simple amenities of our lives in North America, such as outlet coverings. They aren't very expensive. They aren't difficult to install, but for some reason, they had not yet been considered as necessary in this apartment.

When the damp cloth in my hand met with the open electrical outlet, a jolt of electricity shot through my arm, straight past my elbow, across my chest and stopped abruptly at my heart. I didn't feel my heart stop. No. It wasn't like that, but there was an electrical charge in my chest. The tingling continued to run up and down my arm, and across my torso.

I think I screamed, but I don't remember. Maybe I laughed. All I remember is the feeling of electricity shooting through me.

I dropped to the edge of the bed and sat laughing, trembling with energy. I laughed quite uncontrollably for a very long time. There was really nothing funny about it, but I was hysterical for half an hour. When the realisation hit that I was still alive (this took a few minutes) I decided that the cleaning was done and over. We needed a break before one of us got killed.

It would have been a *really* dumb way to die, all things in my life considered.

In that brief, shocking moment, I thought about everything I had done in life, what I had already lived, how I felt about turning in my skin right at that moment, and of course, about the things I hadn't yet done and the people I still wanted to be with. It is amazing that a slight brush with crossing over from this life into the next makes you consider all those things in one single contained flash of thought.

My life is exactly that fragile.

I am nothing but one weak breath away from the end. I cannot save myself. I have to rely on the one who decides my time, numbers my days, knows the hour of my ultimate departure from this earthly existence. My participation in telling others about him is a day to day privilege.

I am not the one who saves.

The urgency to tell others has the potential to overwhelm and drive us to stress, strain and overworking. We aim to be faithful to a call, struggle to meet demands, needs, and reach out to every last soul. We forget that we too, are fragile. We depend upon a life source that does not come from within and is not based on our own strength and energy. Our own limited energy is easily able to combust and destroy us.

Sometimes it takes for us to be warned of the breaking danger that lies ahead if we do not care for the state our own soul, flimsy life, and frail emotions. We have to slow down before we crash. We must rest before we burn out.

If only we could recognise the signs.

BOTCHED AND BLUNDERING

I'm no Jesus. Anyone who knows me can attest to that. It's not just that I'm a woman, either. I trip over my tongue more than I manage to control it. I insult more than edify. I lean toward scepticism more than I exemplify cooperative, submissive belief. And my driving is far from holy.

I am constantly shocked that God still wants anything to do with me, but he does. It is not because of who I am, not surprisingly. It is because of who he is; it is in his nature to love obstinate people like me and to mould us into something we would never be if left to our own wicked demise. So, when other people can sift through the mess that I am and see the message of something remotely worthwhile, I know that only the grace of God could make it happen.

I felt like I was running out of steam, but there were young people from Canada requesting to participate in the cross-cultural programme. How could I leave them out when I'd gone to such lengths to get the momentum going? So, I did what I thought I should: I pressed on, continued to draw my strength from God, and hoped for a way to regain my own personal momentum. The weight of responsibility to continue with what I had started was caving in on me. As I raced through a busy schedule of teaching, studying and ministry, I wondered, dumbfounded, how I ended up with so much on my plate.

If I could have predicted an earthquake, I would have left room for the inevitable relief work that follows.

One afternoon, during another modular class toward my Education Masters, I leaned over the computer of our visiting American professor to help her with some technical issues. I suddenly felt myself wavering. In that initial split second, I thought it was vertigo. The room rocked to the left, then back to the right again. I had pneumonia twice during my first years in the Dominican, and I experience a touch of vertigo from time to time as a lingering result.

I thought if I could just sit down, the vertigo might pass, but then I looked up. The hanging fans were waving back and forth from the ceiling like palms in a breeze.

That wasn't right. I'd never seen vertigo cause that before.

I realised it was an earthquake. One of my classmates said: It's an earthquake. They all scrambled out of their seats and made their way to stand at the back of the room.

I, on the other hand, bolted like Usain and made for the door. I was at the stairs, ready to get as far away from the building as possible when I nearly ran into the Pastor sprinting up the steps. He took three at a time, a look of controlled panic on his face.

What is he doing!? I wondered, but didn't say anything. Shouldn't we be leaving the building? Getting as far away as possible? Or at least crawling under a desk or table or pressing against a doorframe and staying there until it's over? I'm almost positive you are not supposed to head for the top floor of a swaying building in the middle of an earthquake.

As he slapped his dress shoe onto the fourth floor tiles he assured me it was over and that the building was secure. I have to be honest, in that moment, my scepticism won the battle, but he had my attention in his firm grip and he was telling me square-eyed: *Todo está bien.* Everything is okay. He must have seen the frantic look in my eyes. I reasoned with myself that he'd probably lived through more earthquakes than I ever had. We don't get much seismic activity in Toronto. I let him lead me back to the library.

The rest of my classmates were standing in an awkward line across the back of the room in front of the bookshelves, clutching their arms close to themselves, eyes darting to the ceiling fans, waiting for the swaying to pass.

I was so confused.

The building stopped pitching itself around. The whole thing only lasted a few minutes. The Pastor was out of breath and on the phone, relaying to us that we were feeling the tremors from the real beast, which shook violently just southwest of us in Port-au-Prince, Haiti.

My heart sank concretely in my chest. I've seen the way they build stuff over there.

I excused myself to the hallway to ring my Mum before the phone lines went mad and jammed up with international calls. I didn't want her having a heart attack if she tried getting hold of me later and couldn't get through.

Leaning over the spacious window with a view of the greenery and haze of the city, I told her as much as I knew: in our location, we would be safe. We were on high ground away from the ocean and any threat of tsunamis, and our buildings are made to stand against substantial shaking. I assured her that I was okay and would be okay in the days to come. She hadn't heard the news yet. I told her she would soon. I told her not to watch it because it was going to be bad.

Bad was an understatement.

It was terrible. You couldn't just be an eight hour drive away and do nothing. We had resources at our fingertips. We had hope we could bring.

I rang Wilfrido and asked if he was okay. He was shaken up, literally, since the epicentre was only a couple of hours from his house near the border. We made quick plans to do something for the people we knew along the border and on the other side, people he was having a hard time getting in touch with already.

That's when the phone calls started coming. Nurses, businessmen, churches, everyone wanted to help in whatever way they could. I deferred many people to larger organisations in the beginning until I could get my bearings. Then, once the larger organisations were inundated with so many volunteers and donations that they couldn't organise it all, the little groups started doing what we do best: grassroots stuff, ground-level work, translation, transportation, making sure donations and volunteers got to where the needs were not yet being met.

This all happened during the four months after The Earthquake:

Wednesdays, I usually picked volunteers up from the airport: nurses, pastors, my Austrian friend Ruben, Phil (he'd spent five months in the Dominican on a cross-cultural educational experience), and other people who just wanted to help in whatever way possible.

Thursdays, I packed a van with a boatload of donations: army cots, sheets, towels and toiletries, sardines and crackers, power drinks heavy in B12.

Fridays, I left school when the last bell rang, gathered whatever group was with me that week and made my way to Wilfrido's house near the border. We'd go non-stop all weekend and I'd make it home by about two or three in the morning, just in time to get an hour or two of sleep, shower and be at work again by seven, ready to teach for another week.

Across the border, it was like a war zone without weapons, just deadly chunks of teetering cement and people, and gaping holes popping up in your path where homes and roads once stood. I saw faces etched in terror, loss, pain, confusion, and that emotion there are no words to describe that grips a person and renders them unable to think, speak, move, or live anymore.

That look was everywhere.

I remember people's names and faces all too well. They were desperate. They were unable to cope or be rational. They would not be comforted. Limbs got hacked from bodies in order to save a life. The distribution of IV units got botched because workers were few. The transparent sacs rotted in piles under a scorching Caribbean sun while people died of infection or had the infection chopped from their body. We blundered through disorganisation of too many volunteers and not enough translators. Bodies flopped and stiffened in piles, rotting in the sun like the IV sacks.

Plastic-wrapped coffins were stacked beside wasted water bottles while people died of dehydration.

I ran errands, too, like finding food for sleep-deprived paramedics, or buying a hacksaw for a group of doctors.

I don't speak Creole, but I speak Spanish, English and rusty French, and I can drive. I escorted foreign paramedics through cracked up neighbourhoods, clearing the way through debris and strewn supplies to the nearest hospital.

Once I left the city for the weekend, I never stopped.

I can't tell you everything I saw over there. I don't know how. I don't want to dredge up what I tried to push through to keep going because it would drag me down. It was a weapons-free war zone and it was my every weekend for months.

Millions of dollars came through registered organisations. I shouldered an incredible sense of responsibility to make sure every last penny of the donations I received designated to Relief Work, Haiti, found its way into exactly that work. I can't say the same for all the money from around the world that ended up in the country. Who knows what happened there, but it was a botched mess.

I am almost certain that being caught up in the whirlwind of necessary relief work after the earthquake in Haiti was what set my downward spiral in motion. I don't seek to blame circumstances or participants because that is pointless. Who is to blame for The Earthquake? We could point fingers at generations of pollution that have fouled up our planet causing rifts in the surface and angry seas. There is no relief in blaming others. There is no satisfaction in shifting responsibility to others. We have to be responsible for our own actions in consideration of our current reality.

Who is to blame for my own actions but me? I believe it is important that we know when we have hit a wall, crumbled, and need to step back for a total break, not just a physical one, but one that serves to regenerate emotion, spirit, soul, and body. I hit that wall soon after The Earthquake.

Then, instead of seeing the wall, I blundered along, gracelessly botching things up wherever I showed my face.

For They Shall Be Comforted

The first time I met Sami he was smiling against all the world's judgement and reasoning. His black eyes and perfect white teeth shone against smooth ebony skin. As humans go, Sami was instantly likeable. His smile was genuine through sparkling eyes. His voice was gentle, beckoning. You had to really lean in and pay attention to what he said because he refused to shout or raise his voice. Even Sami's laughter was subtle and non-intrusive.

I picked him up on the corner of a street in Santo Domingo's Colonial Zone where he worked as a tour guide and translator. I can't remember how I knew about him, and for as much as I strain my brain to remember even now, the memory evades me. But how we found out about each other doesn't matter as much as why.

Sami sat in the middle of the seat behind me in the van, between other Haitian friends on their way to visit family or try to find their family amid the debris in Port-au-Prince. He was quiet and didn't say much for the first few hours. There were foreigners in the vehicle too. Once we got to the border, he had his passport officially stamped to ensure reentry on his work visa, then directed me toward his mother's house.

We stopped and left some of the foreign workers at a hospital along the way. Once into the melee of traffic in the city, Sami said: I think my brother and cousin were in the University when the roof fell in.

Have you heard from them?

Not yet.

Maybe you'll find them. Maybe they just can't connect right now.

Maybe. I hope. I pray.

We began a tight squeeze up a narrow street. Eventually, the pavement broke off in a sudden drop. I slowed the van, picking my way through former buildings, careful not to disregard remnants of human life that might be under the rubble. A ghostly dust mingled with the dry dirt of the road and swirled in drifts and the wind of passing motorcycles. Reaching upward at a too-sharp vertical angle on the left, a pastel rainbow of jagged slabs spilled over, partially blocking the through-way.

For the moment, the avalanche of homes was frozen beneath the billowing powder of mortar. More tremors would come, as they had every so often. If I kept the van moving, I couldn't feel them as much, but I saw the evidence of them whenever the road suddenly snapped like a cookie or the roof of another building dropped to the ground nearby. The screams generally gave it away first; they became tired and drained after a while, but they were still full of the terror that something worse might yet happen. I kept the windows shut after a while as a defensive tactic from the dust and smoke, and especially from the crying and screaming.

The road became impossibly narrow as it curved between homes and piles of cement. The valley to the right of the road, where homes had been build intrusively close to one another on precarious ledges, had caved in on itself. My heart caught in my throat. I was moving at a creeping pace and didn't want to ask how much farther his home should be in all that mess. I had to concentrate on driving the van along the tightrope of road. If I dared look right, my vision would have fogged over.

In the silence of the van's interior, Sami's calm (or terrified) voice said: Stop here.

I stopped the van, put it in park. I was hopeful.

Is this your house?

No, but you cannot get to it. The road is gone.

We both stared out the front windscreen at the impossibility of driving any further. He was right. Even a smaller car would be at a disadvantage. He would have to go on foot from this point.

How much farther is your house?

Not far. I can walk.

Call me if you need anything. Anything at all.

Okay. I will.

Sami got out of the van, flashed his beautiful smile, and started the harrowing walk toward his home. I waited until he rounded the curve ahead before making a seventeen-point turn with the van. It was a challenge to get it turned around in such a narrow space; there was an eighty degree drop into a valley of garbled concrete on one side and a simmering pile of fragments on the other.

We had agreed to meet again at the end of the weekend for the ride home. I held my breath for good news about his brother and cousin. I said a prayer of comfort for his mother. At least she would feel some relief in seeing her son home for two days.

I found the grip of pavement again under my tires and went about the insanity of another weekend before meeting Sami again, late on Sunday afternoon. I had to cross the border before 6pm or they would keep us in the country until daybreak — or so went the rumours. We both had to work in Santo Domingo in the morning, so getting stuck on the Haitian side was not an option.

I saw Sami on what had once been a curb and pulled alongside him. There was his smile, bringing so much hope that I thought his news could only be good news. One look in his eyes as he stepped into the van revealed the truth of his tragic weekend. I didn't even want to ask, but my raised eyebrows had already posed the question.

He shook his head, lowered his gaze, and his tears came freely, falling without shame or pause. He sobbed like a child and the van was filled with mourning. We all cried for Sami then, even before we knew the details of his story. We had been surrounded by enough tragedy that it warranted inexplicable tears. Defining a particular agony was not necessary. Life in that perpetual state of emotional exhaustion caused tears without immediate or identifiable reason. Sometimes you just cried because there was crying being done around you.

Death hits you differently after you wade through it on a disastrous scale for a spell.

Once he was able, Sami told us that his brother and cousin were both dead. They had been trapped under the fallen roof of the University. The only thing left to do was comfort his mother and younger brother, but he could hardly even do that. His brother had been his best friend.

What could we do for him in that moment but share his grief?

I left Sami at his place in Santo Domingo sometime after midnight. We prayed together and I promised I'd call so we could make plans for the trip again the following weekend. His mother needed the extra support. After that, I made sure that Sami squeezed in and hitched a ride to Port-au-Prince for the weekends. Along the way, we talked about politics, love, history, theology, God's real presence in our lives in our darkest moments of grief, and we laughed a lot, too.

When emotions are fragile, laughter is oddly within equal reach as the tears. Against the background of relentless sorrow, we craved those shared moments of laughter. It kept us sane. It helped us lean on one another. It made the words of Jesus true: Blessed are they who mourn, for they shall be comforted.

Whenever I saw Sami, usually by chance in the streets of Santo Domingo as we both worked in the area, we spent the first few minutes wiping tears from our eyes. It is a way with us in our friendship that seems strange to onlookers. The fragility of our experience bonds us in that wordless understanding. I cry for his loss. He cries because in seeing me he remembers again that he does not to have to carry his burden alone. Whenever we were caught in a passing meeting with other people in tow, they had to wait for us to get all that out of the way before making introductions.

After the severity of the initial relief work, when we all tried awkwardly to slip back into some semblance of normalcy, Sami and I called each other about once a month to check in. I always asked after his mother and the answer was always that she was doing well, but I know it meant that she was alive and as best as could be, considering her circumstances.

Near the end of my time in the country, he ceased answering his phone or returning my messages. It was not like him at all. I started to get worried. One afternoon, I walked down to the flat where he used to live to see if he was there. I tossed pebbles and twigs at the top floor window until someone came out to talk to me. It was another Haitian, but Sami was not there. In broken Spanish and French, he told me that Sami was no longer living at that place, but he couldn't tell me where he had gone. He didn't know.

*****

I met Joujou at the very beginning of The Earthquake Relief Work. The ground was still shaking that weekend. Joujou stared at me in a way that only small children can do with any acceptability. Her eyes were two black pools of eternal emptiness. She didn't speak and I didn't know if it was because she couldn't find a language in which to communicate, or if she might not actually have a voice.

Joujou needed a voice.

The thing we need most as humans is someone who will speak for us: an advocate. When we have the chance, we should speak up just as Jesus Christ speaks up for us.

When I was about eight years old, I spoke up for a girl in grade school who was constantly suffering under the wicked tongues and quick, rough hands of our classmates. She was not my sister, but the treatment she endured was unjust; I had to do something to stop it. I missed out on making friends with other girls in my class. I gained a reputation for fighting, but there had been an initial reason for it: I couldn't walk by. I really wanted her to stand up and throw a few return punches for herself, but she never did. She just collapsed to the ground, hands loosely gripping her head, bawling helplessly, with no idea at all as to how to engage in her own defence. I thought that maybe her Dad had not taught her how to defend herself as mine had.

I set down my backpack that fated morning and rolled up my sleeves for her sake. I guess being a feisty Irish redhead gave weight to my puny size and loud-mouthed threats. I didn't want to fight, but I saw no other choice as an eight year old.

As followers of Jesus, our sense of justice should be ignited whenever we stumble upon the injustices rampant in our midst. Our God is a God of Justice. If we can't stand up for the weak and voiceless, what is the point in having faith in a God of Justice? Justice and Mercy go hand in hand. As an eight year old, I seemed to know that more intensely than I do even now as an adult. I have discovered that, given the proper training, most eight year olds have the potential to think and act with bravery. Included in lessons on how to run a defensive tackle in the hallway of our house, my Dad trained me well to help others find their voice.

I was calling on that eight year old spirit again as I stepped into the rank humidity of Jimani hospital. I dreaded going in there. On my best days, I despise hospitals, but an overcrowded hospital in the throes of multilingual efforts of Earthquake Relief was the pit of despair for my empathic soul. The people needed a voice; more immediately, they needed lunch.

I had collected Ruben from the airport only days after the quake. Ruben married one of my best friends; I have known Melissa, his wife, for longer than I haven't known her. She called me soon after the earthquake and asked how she could help. She wanted so badly to be with me during that difficult time, but as a mother with two small children, it wasn't possible. She asked if Ruben could be any use and I told her to send him over. I soon understood the depth of meaning that the Apostle Paul intended by sending a precious friend in his place to visit other close friends when he could not go himself.

Ruben was a great encouragement. He brought his natural charm, which is a dry clever wit that refreshes, and a gentle, friendly way with people that made him an instant hit with the locals.

I gathered another couple of friends and we drove out to Barahona and stayed with Wilfrido. We used his driveway to sort donations into single portions for distribution at the hospital. Eunice and Naomi, Wilfrido's Creole speaking sisters-in-law joined our group. Once in Jimani, in the midst of the general chaos that surrounded hospitals at that time, we were permitted to park the van inside the gates, out of the way of the ambulance entrance.

It was a quick, organised offloading into the cramped corridors, and our aim was to give a packed plastic bag to every person we met, those injured, and their family or friends.

The hospital is basic in every sense, and not nearly well equipped with staff or electricity or supplies to handle even its usual influx of patients. The covered sidewalks running around the building were overflowing with moaning, bleeding, desperate people. There weren't enough beds. People were lying on the stained floors until a bed became available. Beds were only being made available as bodies were carted out wrapped in sheets. They arranged the bodies side by side, and stacked when necessary, in the flatbed of a truck heading back to Port-au-Prince. It seemed heartless to want a bed. Many continued sleeping on the waxed cement floor for days.

I stepped gingerly over trails of every bodily liquid known to mankind and gave up avoiding the puddles after a few paces. As I walked, I came across a visiting doctor in need of translation with one of the local staff nurses, so I translated. Shutting down my senses as best as I could in order to keep kind, hopeful responses, I visited every corner of that hospital, ensuring that each person received a bag. It was a snack that might ease hunger between donated rice meals from the volunteer food trucks that were making the rounds.

I stopped to talk with patients, pray with them, ask them if they had made contact with family, listen to their horrors if they were able to share in a language I could understand. One boy lay quietly on a cot in the corner of a room, his half-leg suspended in the air, eyes vacant. The room was busy with medical activity. He was staring at the ceiling. A nurse told me he had come in on the back of a truck with his lower leg crushed and infected. It had since been amputated from below the knee. He didn't have much to say. He had no one with him, but had continually asked for his uncle.

I thanked her for the information. The medical staff left the room. Ruben, Eunice, and I decided to stay with him for a while because he didn't have anyone else. I can't imagine being so young, so vulnerable, undergoing such a traumatic experience, and being all alone.

Bon jou, Hola. We tried a couple languages. He turned his head on the pillow and brought his eyes around to look at us, but his expression didn't change. He didn't likely speak Spanish.

Eunice asked him his age in Creole. He said he was eleven years old. Eleven, all alone, recently had his leg removed; this is trauma. Somewhere in the inner sanctum of my mind I thought that we would have to get through this before we can even begin to think of sustainability and development. Do we ever get through this? Can we ever get over this?

Eunice asked if his family were around. He shook his head. She asked if he was still looking for his uncle and he gave a nod. He said he had come with him from Haiti, but he hadn't seen him since arriving at the hospital. He was sure he had gone back to Haiti without him.

There was no way this boy was going to get up out of his bed and go looking for his uncle in the shambled mess of Port-au-Prince any day soon. My natural instinct was to find some way to care for him until his uncle could be found. It was an instinct I had to repress a lot in life, but especially during this chapter of life.

A little voice reminded me that I had to go to work on Monday and it would be difficult to care for the boy's needs or search for his family while teaching, studying for my Masters, and grading papers on into the night. The voice didn't say anything about maintaining my ministry focus right at that moment, for which I was thankful. It wasn't the time to be reminded of focus, it was time to be right where I was: at the bedside of this traumatised boy.

Traumatisation happens when you suffer enduring shock as a result of an emotionally disturbing incident or a physical injury. Enduring shock has no time limit, and in some cases, it does not have a definitive end. This boy's life would be contaminated with the impact of an unending trauma. I began to realise that mine would also.

Prayer was the only thing and the best thing we had to offer, so Eunice offered.

He stared blankly at us, but nodded without hesitation. Ruben prayed for him in English, one hand on his tiny shoulder. He was receiving a good dose of strong painkillers. For the moment, his every pain was dull. Soon he would feel the shock that followed losing a limb, losing your home, getting separated from your family, being brought to a country where few people speak your language.

Ruben, with absolute sincerity, asked me if they didn't ever find any of his family members if he and Melissa could take care of him. He asked me to keep an eye out for him. In the midst of thousands of nameless, homeless, legless boys, how could I keep track of just one? I nodded and told him I would do my best. It was all we could do in the circumstances. We walked toward the exit in silence amid the chaos. Eunice was tearful. I could tell Ruben was struggling with being helpless.

Ruben knows what it means to be completely at the mercy of God, to be helpless. In Santo Domingo, he shared with my students about how God had graced him with the gift of a beautiful son afflicted at birth with a double cleft lip and palate. He told my students that his faith in God had been greatly challenged as he watched his baby, first at three months, then again a few months later, go through painful surgery. He could do nothing to help as he submitted his son to the care of doctors, watched him be put under the numbing influence of anesthesia, wait with his hands wringing as they sliced and stitched his baby. It required a great amount of trust and faith.

Now, as he thought of this little boy, who did not have parents agonising over the loss of his leg or rejoicing at the sparing of his life, Ruben was inundated with that familiar sense of having his big hands tied behind his strong back. The stuff with little Graydon was all so fresh in his mind, I could understand his desire to rescue this Haitian boy. He responded as any father would: he wanted to protect and defend a helpless child. He phoned Melissa later that afternoon and asked if would it be okay with her if he came home with a new son. Without hesitation, she said she would do what she needed to do to get the house or any papers ready if it came to that. I could sympathise with the desire to help. I prayed that the boy would find his uncle. We would probably never see him again in all this chaos.

On our way out of the hospital, I caught the eye of a young girl lying with her leg suspended by the shoulders of her friends. She was accompanied by another girl and a two guys. They were all probably in their late teens to early twenties. Every one of them looked as though they hadn't slept in days. I wondered how many days I appeared to be lacking in sleep.

The girl with the injury bore all the expression of a stone.

This was Joujou.

For some reason, I stopped and asked if I could pray for these kids. They immediately agreed, crowding around me as though I had that life-giving water right there coming out of my sweat glands and fingertips. I guess I did, no glory to me. I guess that's what made prayer such a soothing balm to the mourners, the confused or the shocked.

Prayer quickly became our first response to every unbearable, irresolvable situation. It generally should be, but when a comfortable lifestyle bathes us in ease, our prayers start to resemble an on-line shopping list that will allow us to maintain our comforts rather than ache for eternal things on behalf of a dying world. There is nothing wrong with living with certain comforts; we need to keep an eternal perspective. Life can be a harsh reminder.

Joujou reminded me that this life is quickly passing, that the most important things are eternal. Gisette, Leroi, and Jean-Jean had taken care of Joujou. Gisette, who was fluent in Spanish, told me what had happened: When the earthquake came, Joujou's house caved in at the back on her parents. Joujou and her sister, Perla, were in the front room. After the earth had slowed it's initial shaking, the boys had heard Joujou's panicked screaming. They immediately began digging through the crumbled mortar toward the noise. It took them five hours to dig her out.

During those five hours, Joujou sat beside Perla's crushed body. By the time they extracted her through the narrow hole they had created in the wall, she fought them; she didn't want to leave her sister's side. Joujou was inconsolable. She wanted Perla out too, but it was dark, her rescuers were tired, the electricity was out, and the flashlight was fading. They needed to get her out and away from the dangerous building because the after-shocks were not letting up. Perla was dead. Joujou did not want to accept that, and they had to wrestle her to safety or she might die, too.

Soon, her hysterics gave way to eerie silence. The silence enveloped her and eventually crushed her spirit just as the house had crushed her family. They tried taking her to the city hospital, but her injuries were not life threatening enough, so they turned her away; they were full, and the staff was already exhausted from the chaos.

They managed to hitch a ride on the back of a pick-up truck heading to the border hospital. They thought they had a chance there to save her leg and the skin on her arms. If they waited longer, she would get infected and she, too, like so many others in the heat of the moment, would need an amputation.

I met them a few days after their arrival. Joujou was non-verbal, almost completely non-communicative, except for a childlike whimpering she occasionally let escape when she became aware of her own discomfort. She seemed to have regressed to a psychological state of infantile safety, but I know nothing about psychology.

I prayed for her. There was little else I could do at the time to help her. She had received medical attention and was waiting for a bed. Even if it had been available, no immediate psychological attention was going to help Joujou break out of her shell. She needed prayer, and much else that she would likely never access. In time, maybe, she might peek through in pieces. Joujou's trauma was so fierce it seemed that she might be one who never recovers.

Gisette had her own story, but she was more concerned with Joujou's well-being than to tell me of her woes. The guys didn't say anything, but kept forcing smiles and shaking my hand. They were nodding as though they understood what we were talking about, but they didn't. They were nodding to the sound of her familiar voice; to them, she sounded like she was pleading their case, telling their story, and their nodding would emphasise visually whatever she had to be saying.

We had to leave after a while. We prayed again, and though Gisette didn't seem to want to let go of my arm, we had to leave. I didn't promise her anything, I didn't know what was going to happen. I told her I would keep praying for them. I didn't think I would ever see them again.

I returned the following weekend after Ruben had gone back to Canada. I went first to Jimani Hospital. I asked around for the eleven-year-old boy, but there was no news. One of the nurses remembered him, assumed that his uncle had come for him, but she couldn't be sure. He was no longer in the bed where we'd first seen him. He was no longer at that hospital. So many people had come and gone in those four days that they could barely keep track. He was just gone.

I crossed in front of a room where some commotion was erupting between a nurse and a patient. I recognised Gisette immediately and stepped into the room. She remembered me, called me by name, and asked for me to help the nurse understand that Joujou was not yet ready to leave. I noticed Leroi standing in the corner, quiet and tired. The nurse insisted that Joujou was fine and could go home. Gisette argued that she was not fine — and here was the real big deal — Joujou had no home to go home to. How could they be kicking her out already? She hadn't uttered a word since the event. She could barely take herself to the bathroom.

I asked the nurse for ten minutes, then I took Gisette aside and talked to her, Leroi, and Jean-Jean about their options. Jean-Jean said he would take care of Joujou. He said that if we could transport her to his house, then he would make sure that she had a place to stay and food to eat. He had watched the way the nurses changed her dressings; if they could get enough gauze and ointment, he said he would make sure to do that for her as long as was needed. We could do that, at least. I had to trust his sincerity. He'd already been in the hospital watching over her for the last ten days to his own detriment. We agreed that is what we would do and I went out to the hallway to find the nurse.

Leroi managed to calm Gisette's nerves. Jean-Jean sidestepped her bouts of irrationality, but Leroi dove right in with firm care. I don't think she had slept much since the start of this nightmare. She had extreme emotional fatigue. It was traumatising and everything seemed to be getting worse as the days passed and hope was crushed with every setting sun. Extremes were going around. The most common responses were to either shut down or fly off the handle. Balanced emotions were becoming rare, but it was generally accepted that emotional balance no longer existed.

I convinced the nurse to give us a wheelchair. She was eager to get one. I think she was that desperate for the bed that she didn't mind losing the chair. Jean-Jean wheeled Joujou out to the van and they helped her in while Gisette gnawed at the skin around her chomped fingernails. I was right in assuming that she did not want to head back to that war-like zone in Port-au-Prince. She hadn't shut down like Joujou and her mind was spinning with the possibilities that might await her upon her return. She was nervous, defensive, emotional, and suspicious of everyone.

Once they finished accommodating Joujou in the back of the van with Jean-Jean, Gisette and Leroi sat up front. He let her crush his hand until his fingers were grey as we drove back to their disintegrated neighbourhood. She chattered on in her afflicted Spanish about disjointed topics, and cried and laughed at incongruous spots in the conversation.

I asked her about her childhood, about anything that took place before this rift in her thoughts had jarred her ability to converse sensibly. Her life, however, as with most Haitians, hadn't been very pleasant from the beginning. With a Dominican father who lived across the border and a Haitian mother in Port-au-Prince, Gisette had spent her childhood divided between two parents, partisan to two nationalities who were visibly not best friends, dividing even her speech into compartments of familiar foreign languages.

She sat quietly for a short while as we entered the city limits; the sight shut me up every time.

Joujou was asleep in the back seat, Jean-Jean had his arm draped protectively across her. Leroi began to give me specific directions to get to their street in a calm, measured French. As we squeezed the van through another tapering street, Gisette finally spoke up again:

When the shaking began, and the wall fell down, I got knocked out. When I woke up later, I don't know how much time had passed, but I looked up to the roof and the clouds and I said to God, if he even exists, if he would even listen to me, that I want to know him and give him the rest of my life. I told him I was sorry for everything wrong I had done. I begged him to save me.

She sighed. The thought of any god listening to her seemed impossible, especially the greatest God of all the cosmos. Why would he give her the time of day? She had faith that he would, though, and said:

I don't know where to start; do you know how to talk to God?

I thought about that for a brief second. I might know something about that, yeah.

We stopped in front of the half-collapsed block that used to be Gisette's house. A vacant property sat to the left of the fragmented building, but it wasn't exactly vacant, as it had been a group of houses only ten days previously. It was now a mountain of broken cinder blocks and bent iron rails.

Her brother sat in front of the house, leaning back on a plastic chair, guarding what was left of their home. When he saw her, he stood from his chair and greeted her with a solid hug. She clung to him with intense desperation for a long minute. He gave Leroi and Jean-Jean each a firm hand grip and chest-press and his expression relaxed. They didn't say much. Gisette cried. Her brother did not cry. His face was stone, but for the upturned lips as he shook my hand and said hello with an upward nod that seemed obligatory.

We didn't stay. Gisette grabbed a few of her dust-drenched belongings. She hung off her brother's neck in a lingering farewell before getting back in the van. We wove through the streets until Jean-Jean's directions took the van where it could not proceed. We stopped. This was apparently the place.

They seemed to know what to do without having to communicate. They lifted Joujou carefully out the side door of the van, placed her in the wheelchair, and pushed her across smashed cement, strewn gravel, and the cracked dirt of the street into an enclosed open-air patio.

Moments later I heard my name and looked up to see Jean-Jean standing on the open ledge of a slanting second storey floor. He gave me a scare up there, but he wasn't alone. I asked him to please come down. I could push that building over with my index finger.

They explained that they had managed to clear away the debris, but that the wall facing the atrium had collapsed, and the building sunk down at an angle. They assured me it wasn't going anywhere else. I'm sure they did not think any of it could break off in pieces and slide into the earth the way it had only a week or so previously. I had no confidence in any of the structures around me.

(To this day, I don't hold much faith in physical structures. Sometimes late at night, when everything but the blowing wind is silent, I can feel my house shuddering and I know exactly where I'll jump first if I need to seek protection. We don't get many earthquakes in Toronto, but the lasting physical memory of incessant vertigo lingers at the edge of my weakened sense of stability.)

Jean-Jean descended from his perch and joined us in the dirt of the atrium. I asked him about Joujou, who was staring at us talking with the blank look of a child unaware. A few women from the house (I use the term freely; this was a lone standing room in the rear of several crumpled walls and angled tiers over vulnerable open spaces) had emerged and began to fuss over her, and she let them pull at her, squeeze her cheeks, and inspect her bandages. Jean-Jean looked to Joujou and back to me with a smile. He promised in his best broken French:

I will take care of her. Don't worry. You go. Keep doing what you have to do.

I could only nod. I waved to Joujou and she waved back with the hint of a smile. It wasn't right, though, because it looked more like something that would come from a shy preteen meeting Mickey Mouse for the first time. It was as out of place as Gisette's unnerving laughter. I got back in the van and we made our way toward the border.

Gisette held Dominican citizenship and had decided to try and restart a life nearer to her father, in the Dominican Republic. We drove back to the city. I talked with a friend who also happens to be the manager at a small hotel, and we were able to make arrangements for a few days until I could find a more semi-permanent situation at a small apartment.

Within ten days I found a place behind the *Bohemia* brewery. That worked for a matter of weeks. Every day, I would hike out via *carro publico* to visit, bring food, pray together, and get an update on the job hunt. It wasn't going so well. Gisette was suffering from internal physical ailments and serious psychological repercussions. She needed more help than I could give her, so I talked to a couple of my doctor friends. Eventually, she was on the road to physical recovery. Mental recovery looked less promising each day.

On weekends, I returned to Haiti, sometimes with doctors, nurses, and various other volunteers. Gisette and Leroi came along to visit family on one occasion, and I think that is when Gisette realised that they weren't going to make it in Santo Domingo. She made an honest effort, but the psychological wounds were not healing the way she'd imagined. It would be better to be home, despite circumstances. Being so close to home, and living so disconnected, was burying her in a pit of repetitive debilitating memories. She felt like no one could relate to her and she had trouble controlling any of her emotions.

The few times I had an hour to spare while in Haiti, I navigated the skinny streets to Jean-Jean's neighbourhood to see Joujou. She looked much the same as when I first saw her: completely shell-shocked. If Gisette was struggling, Joujou wasn't even bothering to acknowledge the struggle. She had removed herself from reality and found a place to hide in plain view. Her physical wounds were healing nicely, thanks to the kindness and care of Jean-Jean. Her emotions were suppressed and only childlike whenever they did surface.

Jean-Jean smiled meekly as he explained about her irrational temper tantrums, shrugging them off with an understanding as to why she had become non-verbal and repressed. His patience was inspiring. I reminded myself that he had pulled her out of a hole while she was clinging to her dead sister. He had great sympathy for Joujou.

Gisette gave up the losing struggle after four months and headed back into the mortar piles of Port-au-Prince to be with her family. She called to tell me that she had failed. How could she see her efforts as failure? She cried and apologised. I disagreed; she had done well, made a great effort at starting over, but things hadn't worked out. I encouraged her to keep trusting God in her newfound faith. I said all the right things that should be said.

It is easy to say those things, but much harder to hear them for myself. I compared my garbled memories to the life of Gisette or Joujou; I didn't lose a limb, a family member, my home. At any time, I could have left it all and returned to the land of my citizenship where there is hope and promise. Somehow, though, the debilitating memories — the ones I can piece together, at least — are a lot stronger than I imagined. To compare between my experience and Gisette's is about as effective as comparing birds to laptops. There is no comparison.

When you have two completely unique denominators and variables as different as night from day, the experiences are many, but to compare them is inane. I felt I had no right to grieve, in comparison to the horror they had suffered, so I denied myself the mourning. I marched on with life in detached discomfort.

In the meantime, in the turmoil, Gisette's body healed. She and Leroi welcomed their miracle daughter into the world. They named me her godmother. The new life of this baby girl has brought inexplicable joy to a mourning community knee-deep in the rubble of sorrow. In ways only God could orchestrate, they are being comforted, just as he said they would (Matt. 5:4).

A Chance for Healing
Shoved Under the Carpet

My last trip across the border was very different from others before. There were only three of us and when we crossed over, the chaos had settled. There was something else, too, we could *feel* it.

On previous trips, you could definitely feel something: panic, terror, the slime of a thousand demons swarming about, hissing from a reserved distance at what they cannot touch or harm.

This time the air was clean, the sun was gentle, and there was peace. The peace brushed strokes of white across the landscape; families dressed in pure bleached white linens were pouring out of chapels along the road, crowding into the streets, and the peace spilled over.

Peace carried us gently through calm and polite traffic all the way to the city. It led us to the square in front of the Presidential palace, broken in half like a massive vanilla wafer in the hands of a cosmic toddler.

We stepped out of the van. The ground was shaking, trembling, but it wasn't an earthquake tremor. There was a massive noise and an incredible horde of people in our path, but peace was here.

We walked purposefully into the crowd, unable to hide our smiles, unable to hold back tears, unable to suppress the joy that was filling our chests and bubbling over. The people were crying and dancing, laughing and shouting jubilantly. They were singing, *Jésus est le Roi de notre pays, Jésus est le Roi de Haiti.* Jesus is the King of our country, Jesus is the King of Haiti.

All over the country, men were listening to one another, and women shared their belongings. Haitians were acting with kindness and helping each other. Love was spreading across the nation like a blossoming flower.

It is how I remember it; it is the last memory I hold onto from the time I spent doing what I could to help a number of Haitians get back on their feet, find their families, or start new ones.

I didn't go back to Haiti after that. It wasn't the only thing I was doing with my time and I needed to step back. I had to realise my limitations. I had to focus on the things in my life that were already in motion.

The time of cholera followed shortly after and I tried not to watch the news, but in my mind I saw bodies piled up in the streets for too long. The subsequent tropical storm didn't help the hygiene situation. I remember watching people stack bodies into the back of a pickup truck at one of the hospitals. They were bundling them in soiled bed linen rather than using the available pile of plastic-wrapped coffins for some reason. I'm sure they were taking them back to be identified, but then they were laying in the streets for so long it was dangerous.

By the time cholera made it's way across the border, I had been to Asia and back with a team of Dominican students. No one had forgotten about the situation close to home and for some, their time in Asia meant that they would be more involved locally.

For others, it meant that they would change the entire focus of their career goals and make plans and decisions that would eventually take them back to Asia.

As for me, I was a total wreck, running on adrenaline and about to psychologically implode. I had hit a very serious wall and needed to stop.

But I just shoved it under the carpet and kept going.

Not Enough Porch Time

If I had a list of favourite people, Sister Ana would be somewhere near the top of my list. She is no meek and mild Mother Theresa, but she's got the same spirit. She drives a four wheeler with ferocity, handles a cell phone like a fifteen year old, and has third-world nursing skills that make me shudder. She sometimes lets her tongue go over to the dark side, and in-or-out of Habit, she is all Dominican.

I first met her when I brought a team for a visit to the Leper Colony just outside of Santo Domingo. I got completely lost, which is not surprising, and had to call her several times to get redirected along the journey. When we finally arrived, she was still there. She waited for us with a sincerely welcoming smile on her lips, but didn't hold back from taking a light hearted stab at my lousy sense of direction.

I liked her already.

We stayed for hours visiting, then gathered outside in the early evening sun under the towering trees for a long chat with Sister Ana and Renato.

Renato is a polyglot with an international library in his head. He has lived through wars, disease, and poverty, and recalls all his hardships as exotic character building escapades.

After that, I visited as often as I could just to sit with Sister Ana and listen to Renato recount the capers of his near-century lifetime. Sometimes, I brought groups along if they were in the country. It was always such a celebration of life to see the residents sharing food and laughter with a bunch of young Canadians. I lived for those clock-stopping hours.

We have good relationships in several locations. Participants partnered in service to the communities: Self-Worth Conferences for young women, numerous children's programmes, and whatever else was already happening in the neighbourhood. In the midst of all the locally sanctioned projects were the people and relationships we value, and our love for Christ. That was always at the centre of everything.

There were times I took weekend trips just to spend time hanging out with people. The youth I volunteer with call it Porch Time. Porch Time usually consists of a few hours taken to stop, listen, play cards, laugh, tell stories or jokes, and simply be in each others' presence.

There is such an insatiable drive to be responsible to the pressing needs around us, that often, missionaries don't take adequate time to just hang out and enjoy life and people. I could write books about the things I saw and the projects that sprang up: housing, roofing, church buildings, water purification, education, theological conferences, children's programmes, thousands of dollars in clothing and appliance donations, and the list goes on. The participants kept coming, eager to get involved. To organise it all was a full-time job.

The Apostle Paul says that all the gifts of the spirit and abilities of the church are fantastic, they are essential to building up the church, but without love, they amount to nothing (I Cor. 13:1-3). Love isn't the same as Doing Amazing Stuff for people or even performing miracles. Love, as Paul puts it, seems a lot more like Porch Time; it values time with people with no rush or schedule or thing at the centre other than the people we're spending time with right then and there.

Sister Ana is a pro at Porch Time. In the midst of scheduling, caring for residents, and organising the rest of the nuns in her project, she knows how to stop and waste a few hours on The Porch.

As the opportunities kept appearing, I sat on the proverbial porch with people a lot less. I hardly had enough time to get in five hours rest each night. It was the road to burn out, and I was doing all I could just to make it through until summer.

In the Autumn Season of 2009 I was teaching a full course load of seven different classes in a Christian High School, in the midst of studying a Masters of Education, prepping a team of Dominican students to go on a cross-cultural educational experience to Asia, and providing extra care for a few international teachers. It was already enough, but in January 2010 The Earthquake hit and swallowed years of emotional energy in a few intense months.

I vaguely remember having a few hours of Porch Time, but as I sat in the rocker in front of Wilfrido's house between whirlwinds, I fell asleep to the chatter around me.

I was glad to get on a plane to Asia in the summer of 2010, because it meant I would have to halt my personal involvement in relief efforts that seemed to be getting nowhere.

Adrenaline kept me going. I was so used to pushing the way I felt under the invisible carpet, that any small amount of stress was bound to make me snap. I was a shell of the person I used to be. I was beyond burnt out and I either didn't know it or didn't recognise it, but I kept moving and trying to keep an eternal perspective. I leaned heavily on Christ. I prayed and trusted that he would get me through the days as they scraped past.

A new school year began, and with it came the promise of a renewed spirit. It felt fresh, but short-lived, like a peppermint candy turned stale in its disintegration. It was a briefly effective façade. I pressed my Shell-Self forward in hope of a positive break-through.

In March, I got excited that maybe that break-through would arrive with the group from home. They would come for ten days and participate with Jorge and friends in Pedro Brand. I was looking forward to having them around and hoped for some encouragement.

They showed up with news that a Significantly Influential Leader in our church had caused a rift in my supportive community. They gently unfolded the whole deal over a couple of meals and late night chats. Rumours and doubt had circulated about my vision and mission. It broke my already weakened spirit. I felt abandoned and mistrusted. It was so disheartening that I considered withdrawing my membership from the Body of Christ. I faced a dilemma, though: how do you show Christ if you aren't part of him anymore? I still wanted to be with Jesus, but I *really* wanted a lobotomy that could remove me from the rest of the self-destructing organism called Church.

I wanted to talk to someone about it, but my conscience kept me from mentioning anything to other church leaders and pastors at the time. I did not want to use any good relationship to create bias. I did not want to generate gossip while enduring the destructive sting of wagging tongues myself.

I could not understand what I had said or done (or not) to cause doubt about me and what I do. I had made my best effort to be transparent over the years. I had written honest letters home and they were available for anyone.

The worst part was not knowing exactly who started the talk in the first place; the leader was relatively new to the church and didn't know me. We'd never even had a conversation. I was already overseas when he came into his position. I couldn't understand how he could have formed opinions about me when he didn't even know me.

I wanted desperately to defend myself, but I was so shattered from the activity in The Year of The Earthquake that I didn't have it in me. The more I thought about it, the more I wondered if it was even worth defending. If my reputation could not stand for itself, what was its value? I didn't want to waste time worrying over the issue. Fighting for myself and my reputation would only make matters worse. My best option was to let God deal with the whole situation in his time. If ever.

That sounds like an easy way out. It was anything but easy to hold back from defending myself. I'm good with words. I could have easily talked my way out of it, but it wasn't the right response. I had to keep my mouth shut, so I guess it was a good thing that I didn't have any energy to speak up.

The Youth Pastor had resigned as a result of the whole ordeal three weeks before he was supposed to arrive with our group. It was completely disheartening to know that the body of believers I call my own were being torn apart by gossip, rumours, division, and acts of self-righteousness and un-love. Hate is such a harsh word. We don't have hate in the body of believers, do we?

I refused to believe it. I found ways to forgive and press on, but the thoughts wouldn't leave me alone. When I had brief moments to myself, mostly as I was driving around in city traffic, I had time to think. All I could think about was where and how I had gone wrong.

In the midst of my internal struggle, amazing things were happening around me because God is amazing. The small group that brought the unfortunate news became an encouragement to my broken spirit. Through sweat and smiles, they left a permanent impression of love on Pedro Brand, too.

Jorge was inspired in his work with the community. It had been a dark phase for him, and the pending threat that he could lose his ministry was sucker-punching his sense of reason. These Canadians showed up and gave new life to what he thought was lost. Each morning, when I left the team in Pedro Brand, Jorge would meet us with the energy of a kid at an amusement park. In the afternoons, when I collected them after work, he was still flying. With my heart so heavy, it was a relief to watch his renewed joy. He had a hard time hiding it; their visit had been a colossal pick-me-up.

One afternoon, as I drove out to pick up the team from across the city, I was thinking about all the messiness of the church situation. It struck me as to how awful we must look to the world around us: unloving; full of discord, selfish. Somehow, I could still run on a supernatural stamina despite my broken heart. That tenacity kept me driving in crazy traffic, hosting the youth from Canada, teaching with passion and conviction about the truth. It had to be supernatural.

I was gassing the van down side-streets, trying to beat the traffic across the city. I looked forward to hearing from the group about the wonders and blessing of the day. I wanted to see Jorge's smiling face.

And then I got shot at.

I had just turned left. Two women were carefully tottering up the side of the street in stilettos when a guy jumped in front of them. He started waving a gun and yelling and pulling at one woman's purse strap. He fired the gun into the air. The woman fell to the pavement. He grabbed her purse and started making a run for it, right across the street in front of my rental van.

It all happened in seconds.

I slammed on the brakes to avoid hitting him.

Out of the corner of my eye, I saw a motorcycle to the right and I thought he was going to stop and help. Silly me. I realised he was not stopping, so I decided to hit the thief with my van and deal with it later.

I slammed on the gas. He was only a couple metres in front of me. I was sure to hit him, but then he turned and aimed his gun at my windshield.

I ducked. He fired. I kept my foot to the floor and hoped I would hit him. Hard. It wasn't a very loving response, but it was my knee-jerk reaction.

I didn't hit him. My forward vision was blocked by the dash board, but from the passenger window, I saw him jump on the motorbike. They raced off down the street ahead of my van. On the way, he fired the gun once more, this time at the armed security guards in front of an English school. The guards ducked, but didn't retaliate. He was a terrible shot and completely missed. He might have been firing blanks.

I wasn't sure if I should ram the bike or back off.

In emergency situations, it feels like all the myriad stuff that usually clutters my thoughts shoves off in a haze to the periphery, gathering at the edges. My mind hones in with tunnel vision on the immediate situation and I get a quick picture of my options.

I decided to back off. There was no battle between Justice and Mercy going on in my mind. I wasn't trying to do the most forgiving thing, I was only concerned with my immediate safety and getting out of that situation scratch free.

I eased my foot off the gas and slowed down, putting some distance between us as they headed toward the end of the long street. It was then that I considered the biker might be in on the robbery. It made sense. I wasn't absolutely sure until I passed him at the end of the street, perched on his bike, counting his cash, helmet pushed up on his forehead. He locked his gaze with mine in defiance. I was absolutely sure then. I glared at him from behind my sunglasses.

A wave of regret shot through me that I hadn't acted more aggressively. I should have rammed the bike at full speed when I had the chance.

It was an ugly thought, but it was intense and I gave in to the ugliness of the occasion.

I made a left down another street, then a right, and merged with the public cars heading west.

As I drove along the Autopista Duarte, all the other stuff dropped in from suspended thought at the periphery of my mind, all the dangling thoughts about church family and dodging insane traffic and grading papers and organising dinner for the team in waiting. The Emergency Moment had passed. I was back to juggling the impossible of the everyday.

I can understand why some people would want to live in the sharpened focus of the Emergency Moment. All other things get held in suspension, unable to crowd the mind, incapable of overwhelming you when all you have to consider is the Here and Now. It is a desirable place to be when the stress of everything else presses in. I couldn't live there, though. I'd had enough of that in the previous year. I was pressed under the weight of the people, things, projects, and responsibilities that had longer-term implications. They had only hovered around the edges momentarily. As quick as the event had happened, it was over, and once again I was drowning in my thoughts.

The discouraging lack of support from the church leader made me feel abandoned; it made me feel that getting shot at was a far more containable, and potentially preferable situation.

As a significant spiritual leader in my support community, we looked to him for guidance, instruction, and provision of spiritual leadership. Those rich in faith had received years of discipleship and had developed character through many trials; they would be okay, hopefully. What about the people on the fringes? or those who had new faith? or the ones still caught in the snares of legalism, trying to adhere to a strictly religious life? I wondered if there were people in our little body who were spiritually starving. I wondered if they had become jealous or envious of the liberty and faith of their brothers and sisters. I wondered if they had fallen into the desperate act of robbing the joy of freedom and salvation from those who gave freely. Had they condemned the good works of the righteous brother? Were they spreading doubt about pure hearted sisters?

I wondered again about my split-second judgement of the purse-thief. Would it have been so terribly wrong for me to slam the van into his boney little body? Oh, I thought, God, in his perfect holiness, shows mercy to the wickedest of mankind. My heart sank at how terribly unlike God I am. I wondered why that skinny, dirty, poorly dressed man felt the need to rip a woman's purse from her shoulder in the first place. How desperate do you have to be to attack a woman in a skirt and stilettos? Right, I realised, God's system of provision is so unlike our faulty and corrupt systems of government and religion.

The thief on the cross recognised Christ for who he was and was granted access to the presence of God the same day of his death. I am not The Judge of Mankind. I have been given the gift of forgiveness. I have the privilege of sharing that gift of forgiveness with *everyone* else.

Even the thief on the motorcycle flinging a gun in my windshield?

Yeah, even that guy, ~specially that guy.

I thought about Christ's sacrifice for people like me, who would strike a guy with a van, and people like the leader at church, and people like the skinny thief, and the woman he robbed, and I realised that I'm not ready to die for anyone, yet, not even in my sleep. Thankfully, Christ died for me. It makes me want to live my life for him.

Christ must be at the centre. I thought that Christ was at the centre for me, but it seemed that others were saying he was not, and they claimed that he was at the centre of their stuff. I had to step back and wonder which one of us was deceived. I was willing to admit that it might be me. I had to stop what I was doing, so that truth and love could emerge. I needed some time to rekindle the love.

By the time I joined my team on the other side of the city, I was shaking. I wasn't sure if it was because of that close call or the other thoughts that were pressing in: thoughts about piling responsibilities, my horribly unloving character that responds with such quick judgement when put to the Emergency Moment test, and the niggling temptation to just lay down somewhere and fall asleep until the Second Coming.

I told the group what happened and they sat in silence for a while. I drove in silence.

Over the years, I had acquired the skill of traffic weaving like any good Filipino or Dominican, so driving was something I could lose myself in quite easily. The quiet chatter of the excitement of the day started slowly in the back of the van, and soon, they were reflecting on the joys of their experience that day, sharing stories about their wonder and awe of God as he moved in their midst.

Andrew's voice spoke up beside me. He was praying. Without pretence or introduction, he reached across Laura between us, put his hand on my shoulder, and prayed. It was like he had taken one of those eucalyptus heating pads and wrapped all my aching emotions in it, and I let my tears roll out freely in relief. It wasn't about the shooting or the thief; I wasn't scared and didn't feel threatened. In Andrew's voice, it was as though God said: *I know you. I know the wickedness of your heart. I love you anyway. I will always love you. It doesn't matter if no one else ever does, but just in case, here are nine people right here, and they do, too.*

The tears made it difficult to see the reckless driving around me.

Peace surged through my body at a rate kindly slower than electrocution. It steadied my heart. I was glad the nine were with me right then. It was good to know I had a strong base of support in these people and many others at home, regardless of what went down in their midst.

I did a lot of thinking once that group of awesome brothers and sisters returned to Canada. Maybe it was me: had I stopped making it about Jesus? I considered that for a long time but I couldn't say it was true. Maybe I was just too busy; there hadn't been a whole lot of Porch Time involved since The Earthquake.

I pressed on with all my responsibilities and a sense that my home-foundation had been pulled out from under my feet. I felt less like myself and became more overwhelmed by stupid little things, like the colour of my coffee and if there was a staff meeting I forgot to remember that afternoon, or internally obsessing over the way people looked at me. I was so unlike me, that after a while, even I was sick of my own company.

I wondered how anyone, even God — especially a perfect God — could want to spend any time with me at all.

I stopped going to church because I didn't want to pretend to be the me that I used to be when I didn't have the energy to be me anymore. I stopped going to social activities and whenever I did, it was usually after a sapping internal argument, resulting in dragging myself to whatever it was that I would have otherwise happily avoided.

I stopped visiting the Leper Colony. I stopped going to Barahona and Consuelo and Pedro Brand. I tried to stop thinking about Haiti. As a single woman on foreign soil, I was alone. Outside of enjoying my work, I spent very few hours in public. I felt that whatever that leader and whoever else had mistakenly wondered about me before had now become true.

I prefer sticks and stones and broken bones.

I was emotionally broken and needed some serious fixing. I had a lot of responsibilities to complete before I could tend to that brokenness, but I recognised that something about me was broken. That was at least a start.

Then I brushed it under the proverbial carpet and kept going.

Alone Time with Jesus

If it hadn't been for some very good friends, I probably would have hid in a hole for the rest of my life. Things took a nose dive anyway, no matter how much intervention transpired.

When you're single and living overseas, you'd think finding time for God would be an easy thing, but the way I'd filled my life to the brim and overflowing with doing fantastic stuff, there wasn't any room to be alone with anyone. Once I stopped, time alone was nothing but lonely.

John 15 is probably the most well-read page in my Bible. It is Jesus' final conversation with his closest friends. He sums up the number one thing in a single commandment: Love one another. He starts by telling them that they will not even manage to do that simple thing if they try to do it on their own strength. The fuel is intimacy with Christ.

Jesus says, "Remain in me, and I will remain in you. For a branch cannot produce fruit if it is severed from the vine, and you cannot be fruitful apart from me" (John 15:4 NLT). He uses the illustration of a gardener tending a vine, relating the branches and the fruit they produce to the organism of our relationship with God through himself (Jesus Christ). He emphasises how a close relationship will produce good fruit, good works, that flow out of God's love. It's one of the ways we come to the theological conclusion that we cannot make ourselves righteous by our own efforts; we cannot act in righteous or loving ways if we try to do so out of our own stinking humanity. We need not only to be restored to the vine and tended by the gardener (the Father), but we need to *remain* there.

To remain is an act of permanency, 'a choice to act in a way that daily, hourly, minute by minute, we stick ourselves, our thoughts, words, actions, beliefs, body, soul, heart, and mind, to *that* vine. If we do that, we will be able to love one another. From that love, we will produce fruit that *lasts*. Without the permanency, we are left with nothing.

Sometimes the vine flows so wonderfully and we get branches that produce so much fruit that the poor branch is bending, threatening to break with the weight of lavish grapes clinging to their source. To save the branch, the gardener prunes the fruit down. He diminishes the overload to something more manageable so that the branch won't snap and tumble into the dirt. He clips part of the fruit away, and the branch can bounce, relieved, back to a healthy bundle and continue to produce more fruit in the future.

If left to itself without the pruning, the branch would eventually break off and fall to the ground, destroying all the fruit it had produced and severing itself from the vine. It will need to be grafted painstakingly back into the vine and withheld from producing fruit until even the tiniest tendrils have completely bonded and the scars are swallowed up in the vine. That takes a whole season.

I talked with God all the time, but I needed some real quality time with him. I needed to cut out all the distractions and just sit.

Daily Devotions were limited to the time it took me to shower. Prayer was worthy of censorship and only happened while doing laundry and dishes. I read my Bible at church during Sunday Services so that I could squeeze in some Bible reading during the week.

There came a time when I couldn't even go to church anymore, but stayed at home and joined the Football Fellowship (at Bedside Baptist where Pastor Sheets weaves a gentle sermon about dreaming our dreams for God). My fellowship consisted of watching a Liverpool football game while listening to an online preacher from the confines of my apartment.

The problem wasn't that I had stopped going to church. The problem was in the reason for why I had stopped going: I got to a point where I couldn't face going anymore because I was afraid that people might ask how I was doing. That happens when people care. I am a terrible liar. I would have had to tell them the truth: _____ (blank stare, open mouth, and a look that said, No Comment, which is a whole lot better than blurting: I don't know, go ask somebody else and care for them and just leave me alone). I was beginning to lose my sense of humour.

After a while, Shower Devos became tear filled rants of agonised hurt, silent yelling at God in the cavern of my loneliness, asking him what he wants with me and if he really hates me so much, well, then the feeling was mutual. So there (punch wall, stamp foot, throw soap, get out of bathtub and retrieve soap, laugh at how ridiculously childish it is to fling slippery soap).

I started taking a pass on laundry time prayers: too public, too messy, not enough time to get through all the issues, even with the excruciatingly slow water pressure in my apartment that turned a half-hour laundry slot into a three hour ordeal. That should have been a hint that someone was trying to get my attention, but I never took the time to notice. I was trying to be thankful that I had laundry facilities and was no longer hand-washing everything with water collected from the spouting leak of the fire hydrant in the street or a communal wall tap.

On the surface, I guess I looked to be handling life well enough. I seemed to be okay. Maybe I was only fooling myself. The people who know me best knew that I was overloaded, emotionally drained, and crashing. One or two even said so. They encouraged me to take a real break. They listened to my inarticulate prattling for hours and maintained a generous sense of humour when mine was splintered and defective. They prayed for me when I couldn't pray for myself because I didn't know how or where to start. Besides, praying just made me cry. I began forgetting my name, that is, forgetting who I really am in Christ, but there was no time for it. Even when there was time, it never seemed like enough.

It should be said that through all this I still believed. I never shut the door on God. I didn't *really* think he hated me, deep down, where it counts. The truth had not changed. I base my life and decisions upon the truth. Even in my moments of greatest despair, the truth defies whatever erroneous concept might be understood in admitting these struggles; I never stopped believing the truth with every ounce of my being. In being chosen to recognise the immense love of God in my life since tenderest youth, there is no way that I can ever imagine denying the truth of his love, though

I may fight with myself about it as an option. I didn't *feel* like it was true anymore, and I was giving far too much credit to my ravaged feelings. My sense of reason was doomed in those emotionally charged internal battles.

As irresponsible as it sounds, we have to stop doing whatever we're doing and go home. Run home. I'm not simply talking about getting on a plane and heading for the destination where you were born and raised. Geographic location has little to do with going home.

You'll see as you near the pathway to home, that our Father is waiting by the roadside with his tunic hiked up to his knees, ready to hug-tackle us before we even get near the front gate. You get to know what being prodigal is all about when you've been extravagant with the good things of God and wandered too far from his storehouses, when you've spent it all up until you're empty and homeless in your heart. Run home. You can be sure that your Father is waiting for your return and waiting to throw you a lavish party with all that never runs out. There you remain: Remain in him.

It seems irresponsible to take off and do nothing for a whole year, but even the LORD commanded that Israel give the land a year of rest every seven years. They weren't allowed to till or plant or do anything on that patch of land for a whole year. It allowed the land to replenish itself and take a break from production for a solid cycle (Lev. 25:1-7). It was reflective of the pattern God instilled at the beginning of creation to work six days and rest on the seventh. Even those who resist the idea of Creation Design have to admit that the pattern makes good sense. I don't know any atheists who deny themselves a good weekend or holiday because they don't believe in God.

A Sabbatical is when you leave the every day grind and dedicate a year to travel and learning. Sabbath marks the seventh day, or seventh year, and is dedicated to intentional rest. It is a fair chance for your overall system to reset.

I needed to leave the travel and sit still for a year.

I overtaxed valued relationships as I fizzled through burnout; my words were unchecked, my emotions were often irrational, and I had the gleaming personality of a speed bump. I am sure that in hitting the skids I left a dark laceration in the wake of my burnout that may never be erased or repaired in this lifetime.

All I can do now is stop and remain for as long as it takes to prune this cracked branch.

I was cooking in the heat one afternoon, music blasting, when I was halted abruptly by the words of a song. The song "Lovesick" by South African duo *The Arrows*, has an edgy, pop-funk sound, and the lyrics are stark truth. It was like a warning bell ringing out in the humidity of my Caribbean kitchen: slow down, breathe, stop being so busy, sit with Jesus.

As the vocalist sang out "I just don't want to feel like this" and hinted at being a tree that needs pruned, I could only agree. The song makes a call to go home, turn off the phone, and be alone with The One we've really been looking for all this time. I had to turn the tables on my compulsion to be involved in Doing Good Things and refresh my dedication to the search for The One who is Good.

I laughed at myself as I sat there in the steaming kitchen, the scent of burnt meat filling the air, and made a promise to run home as soon as I could. I decided to be alone and spend some time sitting in God's presence. I would take a sabbatical year. I would not make any plans to do any more good work until I had a chance to remain in the presence of the Author of all good things.

Jesus said, "Remain in me and I will remain in you … you cannot be fruitful apart from me … remain in my love … your joy will overflow … love one another" (John 15).

I needed some alone time with Jesus.

STARING AT WALLS

I sit and stare at the newly painted walls of my room. Blanched and lacking any real brilliance, a gloss-less flat matte finish, these walls are the colour of caucasians in February.

I think about Seven Years in the Dominican Republic. Like a watercolour in the pouring rain, the memories slide down the canvas of my mind, bleeding colours into transparency until the painting is gone. All that is left is a pool of faded brilliance at the base of a promising white space.

I did more damage than good.

After The Earthquake I drifted so far from my purpose that I think I may never get it back.

These and other such ridiculous thoughts escalate into development of a theory that makes me wonder whether my time in Latin America was a completely botched failure.

Unfortunately, theories are sometimes more believable than the truth. I stare at the walls and start to believe my theories. Sometimes, because it is summer, I sit on the deck in the backyard and listen to music or read fiction and stare at the trees. The trees are beautiful here.

The longer I think about the details of my life overseas, the more intangible and transparent they become. I have no motivation. I have no passion. And I don't care. That is what worries me most. If I don't care, does it mean I never cared? Will I ever care again? Will my memories return to me?

I take my time in the mornings. I stare at the walls for a good hour or so. The ceiling is spotted with a couple minuscule dots of green reminding me of the previous vibrant colour those walls once were. Now, there are careless streaks and splotches of pale Vintage-Jasmine-Love-Letter-White, or whatever this colour is called. My paint job was not as perfect as my father's before me. I have to live with it.

It is the only thought on my mind most mornings as I sit and stare at the walls. I try to gather my thoughts, but they have melted and refuse to be collected and compartmentalised. I try to go back to the nebulous beginning and create a timeline of events, but it's like trying to pull apart hardened gum with greasy fingers. My memories won't cooperate.

Those seven years seem to be one set of inseparable memories. When I try to concentrate on individual events, they bleed into one another and mess up my sense of chronology. Things didn't happen in a logical sequence; they happened according to significance and experience. Sometimes they happened all at once.

In hindsight and reflection, chronology cannot find a niche among these memories. To put them in chronological order is to amputate one memory from a body of others in which it has significance. I have learned first-hand about the repercussions of unnecessary amputations.

I can look back and see a hazy moment when I hit a wall, though. It amazes me that I was able to keep going after that.

I had strong local support that helped me hobble along for a while. Then the crash caught up with me. That's when I stopped going to church, stopped going out with friends, stopped visiting the ministries and the people I had grown to love. Eventually, I stopped moving. Then I came home to stare at walls and trees.

In North America, we are obsessed with fixing things. We see broken stuff and we just have to fix it. We must find a solution. It's part of our DNA as a culture. It can be a really beautiful aspect of who we are as a people, even if we often have to curb the urge to fix others.

I wish people were as easily fixed as the starter in my car or the paint globs on my ceiling. We are tragically not that straight forward. We are infinitely complex. Not surprisingly, the fixing of a broken mind is a complex procedure that takes agonising time. A season of life is a long wait.

I grow impatient with the process. I want to rush it along, but I find that it will not be rushed, so, I stare at my walls. I find a porch and some long-haul friends with a deck of cards and throw down a game of euchre. That helps. I sit on the deck in the warm breeze of a July afternoon. I watch the trees do nothing and be wonderful at it.

I wait.

I wait for my memories to sort themselves out; for my mind to heal; for a return of the me I once was.

I think it might be an hopeless aspiration.

Burn Again …

Jesus said, "The truth is, no one can enter the Kingdom of God without being born of water and the Spirit. Humans can reproduce only human life, but the Holy Spirit gives new life from heaven. So don't be surprised at my statement that you must be born again" (John 3:5-7).

We make it our prayer that God would give us opportunities every day to share his love with people so that they too might be awakened in their spirit to new birth in the Holy Spirit. This is why we keep on doing what we do, no matter what the cost, because the eternity of every human being is at stake. We need to be passionate about our work and we also need to know when to take a break.

But we don't stay down. We aim to get filled up and move forward again, to burn again with the passion of life so that others will be born again in the Spirit.

You used to have a youthful spark that burned for missions. Then you got fried, seared, frizzed: completely burnt out. What happened? You were overworked and gave it your all. You got weighed down by too many responsibilities. You got let down, let go, left out, left behind. You got wise to the harsh realities of life. You felt loss and grief and disappointment, in yourself, mostly. Ultimately, you got older (not old, just older).

That's what happened.

When I think of giving my all to life and burning out because of it, I think of that mythological and mysterious creature, the Phoenix. The legendary bird has a compelling story for those of us who are believers: After a life full of purity, healing and sacrifice, the Phoenix is consumed by fire and becomes a pile of ashes. That is not the end of the story. With great anticipation, after it has been restored under soothing waters, the Phoenix rises to live a dedicated life of healing and sacrifice once again.

When I think of the Phoenix, I think of Job. There is no character in the Bible who could claim burnout more than the righteous Job. He was a man highly regarded by his peers and countrymen, yet everything was stripped from him. He was left in a state of pain and loneliness that few of us will ever see in our lifetime. Job defies what is natural: to complain, to turn his back on all that is righteous, and to curse God. Instead, he speaks well of the God who allowed his wealth and health, and his suffering. When God talks to Job and reveals his grandeur in ways that Job can see, hear and feel, Job covers his mouth and is humbled. God then restores his wealth and influence until his death in old age.

Job said, "I delivered the poor who cried, and the orphan who had no helper ... I caused the widow's heart to sing for joy. I put on righteousness, and it clothed me; my justice was like a robe and a turban. I was eyes to the blind, and feet to the lame. I was a father to the needy, and I championed the cause of the stranger. I broke the fangs of the unrighteous, and made them drop their prey from their teeth. Then I thought, 'I shall die in my nest, and I shall multiply my days like the phoenix; my roots spread out to the waters, with the dew all night on my branches; my glory was fresh with me, and my bow ever new in my hand"' (Job 29:12-20 NRSV). He gave all he had to being a good man in life. His only desire was to burn up and live once more, so that he could do it all over again.

Job shone with the blessing of God in his younger days. From God's blessing he sought to bless the lives of people around him. Then, in a flash, he lost everything. It was literally all burned up in fires. All that remained was his spirit, a wasted body, and his unfailing trust in God.

In the darkest time of turmoil, Job only spoke well of God. So, God blessed Job twice as much as he had when he was younger. Like a phoenix, Job rose up from the ashes even more beautiful and blessed than before.

The Anomaly in Transition

I came home.

I made the great move from overseas to the place where I was raised. It is an alien transition. Finding a new groove in what is supposed to be familiar is confusing and emotionally exhausting. People find it pretentious that I lose my way in the town where I grew up, but the landmarks are new and unfamiliar (when did they put that hospital there?).

Things changed when I was gone. While others might feel that I am trying to impress, I find myself less impressive than a bowl of sugar-free cornflakes.

I immediately missed speaking the language I had become accustomed to; I found it difficult to reach into my native vocabulary for everyday items or activities. How could I forget to speak English? Seriously, that's dumb.

That I took the time and energy to learn a new language, faced great loneliness, set aside my personality until I could grasp the flow of another tongue — that too has become a thing that separates me from my own. It creates unwanted barriers. What do I do with it after I don't have a daily use for it anymore? Mask it, push it aside, put it to sleep? *No tengo idea* ... I don't have a clue.

I tried to reintegrate. There is no manual for how to effectively blend seven years of your life into the bookends of your other life. To me, there does not appear to be an existing division. I am a different me than I used to be, but I am still me somewhere beneath these smouldering ashes. I cannot carve out the pieces of me that are distinctly not the me that fit in this place once before.

I am not a cultural chameleon. I carry with me the marks and habits of the cultures I have called home. The languages and accents I have formed and nourished dance like flashes of sunlight between the clouds in my foggy brain. I cannot reintegrate by cutting those things out. I cannot dissect me to make me fit better anywhere. I am different. I am changed. I must accept that before I can expect others to accept it. All at once I fit and I don't fit. I must learn to live with these ricocheting emotions, facets of my personality, and the mess of languages that knead through my polyglot thoughts to find the right fold of my tongue for the conversation.

It hit me in a way I'd never thought of: single thirty-something women, like me, who have lived overseas for extended periods of time in alternative languages, and then return to a life in their home nation are an anomaly in the North American Christian community. Most people in church community close to my age are married, have a kid or two, a mortgage, and a job they've been plugging away at for years already.

To confirm my suspicion, a long-time friend told me: You are an anomaly, a wonderful one.

I am an anomaly, nonetheless.

I quickly realised that I needed to talk to other people who have already been down this road, or are in the midst of a similar transition. After a summer of staring at walls and trees, outings with my nieces, and reading everything I could get my hands on, I could clearly see the cracks in the frame of my overloaded mind. Fortunately, I have a network I can tap into, and I was able to meet up with some wise friends at varying stages in their dedication to an international career.

I had questions. I wanted to find out how these ordinary people handled doing life alone overseas in the midst of highly stressful situations, stark poverty, and second and third languages. I wanted to know what support or opportunities they had been given by their organisations.

Did they share what I was feeling? Had they tasted the same victories or drank from the same cold lonely cup? I wanted to know that I wasn't alone in all this. I wanted bring understanding to the larger community where we Anomalies engage in our ministries.

In the back of my mind, the thought of failure toyed with my waning courage to speak up and ask my questions. What if I brought up things that carried a world of regret or pain? What if I offended by getting too personal or digging too deep into the past or unrealised life expectations? What if I dragged out issues that had already been flogged, burned, and buried? Worse: what if nobody shared even a glimpse of anything I felt? What if I was the only one?

What if I was truly alone?

I needed to know if I was the entire anomaly.

Stop Spinning your Wheels

I grabbed a plastic chair and dragged it out to the shade of the trees lining the back lawn. The sun shone bright, heating the warm day, but an early afternoon breeze kicked up between the hundred year old houses.

Lila joined me, setting her chair about a metre or so in front of mine.

She was in for the week and I requested an interview. She offered gladly to talk with me about her experience as a missionary, both overseas and since returning home. More than a few years ago, she came home from Asia to care for her parents, a responsibility she still cherishes as her mother has reached mid-nineties.

We've known each other for a while, so I skipped much of the preliminary chat and cut to the chase; "I want to ask you about before you went overseas as a missionary, did the organisation address the issue of singleness, or say anything about it, during your preparation to go overseas?"

Lila shifted in her seat. "Well, I'm sure they did, I guess, but, I don't really remember," she gave me one of those looks that says I've asked her the wrong question. I knew I had. I knew she'd set me right. "But you know, I didn't join the mission agency until I was already in my thirties, and I *did* have a life before that," she laughed.

I could see where she was going. I was relieved that she'd be willing to talk about her life before the organisation. Contrary to popular church belief, we single women don't marry the organisation. Most of us are not nuns. Though, I have been asked on a few occasions (apparently, being a nun is like having a spiritual superpower).

"I didn't grow up as a Christian. I only became a Christian in university," she said, bringing some context to her situation. "I had boyfriends before I knew Christ and it was like, anything goes, you know?" she spread her arms out for emphasis on the anything. "So, when I became a Christian, that was one of the things I had to grow up in. I had to learn what it meant to be a Christian and the affect it had on romantic relationships. It wasn't easy."

I can't imagine the drastic change of mindset that would have been for a twenty-something in the mid-seventies with all that free uninhibited love floating about on university campuses. I suppose not much has changed.

"I dropped out of university after two years and went to Bible School. I not only received theological training, but I also learned about missions and committed myself to a life-time of cross-cultural ministry. After graduation, I sensed God leading me to return to university to finish my degree."

"You studied to be a teacher, right?"

"Yes, an English teacher, and after I finished university, a need for a teacher arose. I suspended my mission application process to fill the need, but I wasn't sure how long I would stay."

I could understand the idea of meeting the need as presented and putting a dream or calling on hold. I could even relate to that personally, but then she said,

"The only thing was that I had become almost too comfortable and my desire to be a missionary got shoved to the back burner." She paused here, mulling over that particular neglect.

"I never intended to do that," she reflected, "but I had reached my mid to late twenties by that time, and all of a sudden I wasn't as eager to go overseas as a single person. There were options, in particular, one man I knew had become a very good friend, and I was kind of waiting around for something to happen."

She put her hands in the air, remembering the wasted time. "Rather than be involved with what I *could* be doing for God, I had started spinning my wheels." I tried not to show it, but she'd just hit a nerve. I leaned forward, my attention focused, thankful for the camouflage of sunglasses.

"This friend I mentioned was on staff at the school. We spent a lot of time together. He knew how I felt and I was pretty sure he felt the same way, but nothing was happening. I started to ask myself how much longer I was going to wait around for this guy, or any guy, for that matter."

I get what she was saying. I don't know a woman who doesn't. So what do we do? Hang around waiting until he decides to act or keep on with the great things life has to offer?

"I realised that if I didn't make a decision to move on," Lila continued, "I could get caught waiting around for a long time. Then again, if I would follow my calling to become a missionary, there was a real possibility that nothing would happen out there either, if you know what I mean."

I knew what she meant: the risk of never getting married would be that much greater if she decided to abandon her life here and chase after the call of God.

"So, I had this conversation with God and I put a stake in the ground right there: Either I was going to keep on spinning my wheels, waiting around for something to happen that might never happen, or," and she leaned forward, elbows on her knees and looked right through my shades into my eyes. "Or I was going to take a step out and trust God that he'd take care of me as a single missionary."

A stake in the ground. It's what we all need. Otherwise known as the guts to be brave enough to do what it is we know we should do, that thing we always really wanted to do, no holds barred, no matter what anyone says or thinks about us in the doing.

A big immovable stake in the ground …

I pictured Lila hammering a twelve foot stake into the Plains of Middle Canada, a determined, satisfied look on her face, the indecisive "friend" standing behind a line of red tape, wondering exactly what had just gone wrong in his life.

She'd decided to stop spinning her wheels, that's what.

"I often went back to that moment in the years that followed, reminding myself of the choice I'd made to move overseas as a single woman and pursue God's call in my life. It was a pivotal moment. Finally, at thirty-one years of age, I was going to follow the call and get on with what God had prompted me to do years earlier." She had initially gone to Bible School to follow that call.

I sat back in my plastic chair again, a sudden chill sweeping in against the warm summer air. The sun was high and we were sitting in the shade, but I'd become used to high and humid temperatures in the Caribbean. I'd only been back in Canada for a month of summer sun. I hadn't adjusted yet.

I remember when I left Canada seven years ago, under much the same circumstances: wanting to pursue the thing that God had put in my heart, to chase after the dream and take wild chances at getting there. I'm sure Lila remembers what a confused and conflicted woman I was back then, too. At the time, she spoke to me of making a choice that I could live with, of taking risks and of counting the cost. She had encouraged me then not to get caught in the cycle of indecision but to take hold of the best years of my life and spend them well for God.

Maybe she doesn't remember all that, but I haven't forgotten her inspiring words or her resolute attitude. During the past seven years of taking my own risks and stepping forward to follow God's call in my life, I have often thought of the choices she made and I've been able to press on.

It's strange how that happens to us as humans; one person suffers and because of their suffering, we are able to overcome our own sufferings. One person obtains victory and we celebrate as though we have completed the task ourselves.

This interview was quickly mutating; my personal issues were surfacing and her words were like balm, soothing, healing, and reparative in a way that may allow me to get back on my feet again. I wanted to hear more of her story.

"So, you were a little older than most singles leaving for the field," I observed. "That probably made a difference in how they treated you or saw you. I mean, concerning my initial question, do you think they probably suspected you were already well-adjusted as a single woman? Perhaps they didn't broach the subject in the same way as with younger applicants?"

"Yeah, maybe," she seemed more inclined toward answering that question, now that she had explained her life before she was a missionary. "Though, I'm sure it came up during the interviews, I just don't remember it, it was a long time ago, you know."

"It wasn't *that* long ago," I insisted.

I have this proclivity of freezing the ageing process of people I know. Somehow, my assumption had locked Lila into the early forties range and in my little mind, she hadn't budged in the eleven years I'd known her.

"Oh? Nearly thirty years!" she exclaimed with a laugh. She probably couldn't believe that I could possibly think that time had passed and yet somehow, she hadn't aged. Oh, yes I could. It's one of my lesser known magic tricks.

"No way, wait, how old *are* you these days?" I asked, unwilling to confess that my magic doesn't work. I have forgotten how to be Canadian; I ask freely about age whenever I can.

"I'll be fifty-nine," she was still laughing at me under a disbelieving smile.

I am ridiculous, after all. I first met my friend Melissa when she was thirteen and though she's changed her hairstyle, has two kids and is in her mid-thirties, I somehow still think of her as the same girl I knew at thirteen. She is, really, just further on in numbers. Lila caught me off guard with that confession, though. She really doesn't look much older than when I first met her. Well, maybe a little. I said the first thing that came to mind:

"Oh man, Lila! You could be my mother."

"Ha!" she already knows me well enough to know I am absurd, so that last statement didn't come as any shock. "Could I, now? Great. Thanks a lot, that's just what I need."

I shrugged and started to wonder where all that time went.

"But speaking of that, I was never a really very maternal type of person," she confessed. I know this to be true about her. "Not that I don't love kids," she quickly clarified, hands raised in objection. "I love them all, all my nieces and nephews, etcetera — I just never really doted on having my own children, if you know what I mean."

I don't. I mean, I understand it about Lila, but I don't know that feeling for myself. I *would* like to have children and I love having them around all the time. I spent most of my youth and young adulthood working with small children. Since I have become older, my tolerance of large groups of children together in small spaces has diminished to zilch, but I cherish those one-on-one times with my nieces and the children of close friends. I would *love* to add my own children to that group one day if God permits. So, when she asked me if I knew what she meant, even though I nodded in understanding, there was a deeper part of me that said, "No way, I don't get it" because maybe that maternal instinct in me still runs strong.

At this point, I think we both realised that the interview had gone way off the tracks and we made a scramble to find our place again. She's much better at that than I am.

"Anyway, I went through the support raising process here in Canada and made it to Asia that next year to start language study."

"So, once you arrived in Asia, did you feel you had a community of support around you? Did you feel valued as a single individual? Were there distinctions made between you and other married colleagues?"

"In the city, during my language study years, there was a good group of young singles in that field at the time, so, no," she shook her head, "I didn't really feel it was all that big a deal, there were others, many others, like me, from all over the world. We did a lot together, as well as having some really close local Thai friends. It was a good start to living in Asia."

"So, you didn't really feel lonely in the beginning very much, did you?"

"Well, our living situation at language school was like being in a university dormitory, so it was like that lively environment. There wasn't much room to get very lonely between language study and church and mission activities. We kept very busy in those first years."

"How long did you stay in the city? Didn't you live in a tribal village?"

"That's right, but before we could learn the tribal language, we had to learn Thai to get by within the country."

"Of course," the tribal villages, though they are somewhat disconnected from Thai life, use Thai as their official educational and trade language, and if Lila wanted to get anywhere in the country, she'd also have to know Thai.

"I was only at language school for sixteen months before I moved up north. It was hard to leave that active environment. It was even harder to start all over again with learning the Karen language and go to live with another missionary in a new area, especially when I had very little choice in the matter." That was thirty years ago, things have changed drastically in the mission since then.

"I was travelling to the village and living in a nearby city with someone I didn't really know very well, so it made for a difficult year. I really just wanted to live in the village, so I wrote a letter," she caught my eye. It was only thirty years ago but the internet did not exist yet, and email was still a long way off. "I sent my letter to the directors asking if it was possible for me to move into a village to be among the people with whom I wanted to work."

"You had to wait a lot longer for deliberation and response back then, I suppose?"

"Yes," she agreed. "Everything went through the mission. You couldn't just up and make your own decisions about your ministry or living situation. There were procedures and long" (she dragged the word out) "processes for the way these things were accomplished."

There was something about the simplicity of life those few short years ago that even I miss, but the use of the internet has brought a dexterity to our existence that I'm not sure we could live well without anymore.

"Well, in the last year before my first home assignment, they came up with a place for me to live in a Karen village," she smiled; the news had been well-received.

"I went to live in the village by myself," she cringed. "It was not an ideal situation. They would have preferred to send me with someone else, but there wasn't anyone else available at the time and it was the best alternative."

All alone in a village in the jungle of North Thailand … I made a distinction between Lila's nun superpowers and mine in that moment, but then, that's the sort of thing people do to separate themselves from the responsibility of following a calling for the sake of the gospel; they convince themselves that the ones who go, the Lilas of this world, have some kind of superpower that is superior to their own. This is absolutely *not* true. Lila just had the courage to step forward and trust that she could draw on God's power when she needed it, and to suffer what may come. I reminded myself that neither of us actually has any superpowers (and neither of us is a nun, that's for sure).

She continued. "It was good for the first while, but it got lonely very quickly," she confessed. "I wanted to be there. I was in the right spot with the right people, but I was all alone in many ways. Of course, at that point I could sort of see the light at the end of the tunnel; I was leaving on home assignment at the end of the year. That made it easier to get through the loneliness in the first year.

"When I returned after a year at home in Canada, I was dreading going back up there all by myself," she divulged.

"Imagining four years in the same situation I'd been in during that first year was too much for me to think about."

"Couldn't you just quit?" I knew it was a stupid question, but I had to ask. To quit would mean an explanation to her supporting communities, another long process of letter sending, discussion as to where else she might go, a change in ministry, possibly a change in language. The option of quitting was not as easy as it sounded, but she had an even better answer.

"I didn't want to quit," she smiled. "I was very committed to working among the Karen people and I didn't want to be re-assigned. I just needed some kind of relief in my living situation. I didn't want to have to write and ask about it either. So, this was an ongoing battle in my mind, apart from all the implications in the village."

"What do you mean? What implications?"

"Well, the question arose about my single status in the village. For the tribal people, it was rare, strange, that a woman in her thirties would not already be married with children. There was great concern among the villagers that I was going to be left all alone in life without anyone to care for me."

"Oh, yes," the light came on, "I know what that's all about." It's a very typical thing in many cultures around the world to be overly concerned for single women, especially ones who have no children to care for them. I had all this fresh in my mind, having just come from seven years in Latin America.

"What about opportunities for a relationship there? With any of the local men or other single missionaries?" I asked.

"Well, I don't want to sound," she searched for the right expression, "partial," she cringed, "but my broad cultural understanding and travel experience was, and is, so different from the people in the village. I'm not saying I'd be against it if it ever genuinely happened, but it didn't, if you see what I mean. Even my work partner in the translation, for the open mind that he had — well, we were just so different in our worldview, and he was far more informed than the average villager. It would have required far more work than I was willing to allocate."

"Any other single missionaries?"

"I was surrounded by married couples and single women in my field," she answered frankly.

"So, it must have been extremely lonely …"

"It was," she stated firmly. "I was four hours from the city and civilisation. I had my motorbike and could go to another village about twenty minutes away where there were other missionaries, though. I made a point to do that to keep my sanity, but it was lonely.

"I would have been your age then. Can we talk about hormones? We're women. There are things that happen to our bodies in our mid-thirties that we can't control and to deal with all that alone in a tribal village was something I could never have prepared for, even though I was apprehensive about my return."

There was that nerve again.

"I would have had a complete psychological meltdown," I blurted. She laughed, nodding. I guess she knew that I kind of did, though I was in different circumstances.

"I almost did," she got serious. "I don't know *what* kept me going. I was just trying to make it through each twenty-four hour period, without cracking up. After that year, my fifth year overseas, I got down on my knees and begged God to do something about the situation. I was desperate."

My mouth was open, my brow creased, as if I too was reliving the memory with Lila. I could relate to her loneliness, that kind of inner agony. I don't think I've ever had anyone else speak to me so bluntly about it before, though. I nearly cried right there in that plastic chair. I think she knew that what she was saying was getting to me, but it was real, it's what she went through.

"I wasn't really praying about it, you know, not really committed to bringing it before God every day or anything like that. When I begged him, I was just desperate for something to give, or I was going to give in. It was a very dark time for me overseas." Lila paused. I think she was waiting for me to digest that truth, that reality, before moving on.

I felt as though she was trying to tell me that I'm not alone.

"Shortly after that," she continued, "the mission asked me to join a Bible translation project. That meant moving to the city again and I was willing to sacrifice my proximity to the village for my sanity," Lila smiled at this like she knew she was speaking right into my spirit, like she could read my thoughts: the loneliness, the pain that it causes, and the very difficult decision to give up one good thing for another.

I sat there like a sponge. Lila had turned my so-called interview into a pick-me-up session, fortifying my spirit and boosting my diminished morale. I was amazed. There were no super human powers she used to tackle the impossible, just an authentic struggle to stay afloat, in the midst of which she took part in the accomplishment of helping to translate the New Testament for a Karen language group.

"Did you go back to the village at all?" I asked when I found my tongue again.

"Oh yes, all the time, but I was also active in town. At church, I made sure to get involved in a small group and make a variety of friends. I'd been holed up in the village for so long I had to make a point of getting out and being social, but it was a good way to end my time there."

At the end of that term, Lila moved home to care for her parents, but she maintained the contact with her Thai friends, especially one who became like a sister during times of extreme loneliness.

"So, after you moved home," I shifted gears in the interview, "how did your church community deal with a single woman in their midst? I mean, did they just give you a five minute slot during Sunday School or what?"

"No," Lila laughed that off. "In the Anglican church, we don't bother with all that complication you Evangelicals deal with all the time."

I snapped my fingers. Of course. I had forgotten that she's Anglican. I remember my days in the Church of Scotland and this struck a chord; the issue of being a woman with a calling is different in Anglican congregations. They are not nearly as uptight about women or even single women in ministry as some communities.

Her transition to life back in Canada was not really very dramatic at all, which also has a lot to do with her laid back personality and not just her laid back church.

"Do you think you'd get married still, if the opportunity arose?" I probed, just curious.

"Sure," she answered quickly, "why not? If the right opportunity comes along. Of course, the Lord will probably have to hit me over the head with a two-by-four before I'd get married at this age!" She joked. "Just kidding. But really, I won't be too upset if it doesn't happen, either. I've lived this long without that kind of companionship."

I thought about living in that state of contentedness. In all the time I have known her, Lila has always talked of her singleness as a blessing from God. She admits to the struggles, but sticks to the declaration that the blessings far outweigh the difficulties. Looking back over her life of ministry, she wouldn't have had it any other way. That is an encouraging attitude and as she shares it with me and other young single missionaries, it inspires us to remember the blessings of the life we have, rather than waste time wishing things were different.

I had no more questions, but she had one last thing to tell me.

"There is certainly a struggle for us as single women, but the blessings of this life far outweigh the struggle. We have to see the blessing in our opportunity to be single for God. I keep going back to that stake I put in the ground thirty years ago, to that pivotal moment in my life. I always remember that I made a choice," her stare dared me, challenged me to consider the choice she made and choices I have made or need to make in my own life.

"I drove that stake in the ground and declared that I was going to move forward with God's call on my life, but before I could truly move into the adventure God had for me, I had to stop spinning my wheels."

WOW. THAT JUST HAPPENED.

As the year progressed, I slid back into things that came naturally. I defaulted to spending time with the teenagers in my church community. They readily accepted my new struggling self without need for justification. They understand that life mars us with its imperfections. In their vulnerability, they offered shoulders of consolation and the innocence of youthful idealism.

Many of the teens and young adults from this group have visited ministries I worked with in the Dominican Republic. They participated in being part of my particular dream as they engaged in a time of cross-cultural experiential discipleship. For most of them, the visit changed their lives.

Steven visited in 2012. Since that time, he has carried a life-changing story in his heart.

I cornered Steven during our winter retreat at the beginning of 2014. I asked if I could talk to him about what happened when he visited the girl in *La Cuarenta*. He didn't need a detailed reminder. He knew exactly what I was talking about.

Outside, a fierce cold winter held Brampton in its clutches, but in our minds, we returned to that day in the Dominican Republic.

As I remember, it was hot. The stifling heat of a Caribbean Springtime mid-afternoon beat the pavement. The refreshment of the ocean was at least an hour's drive away and a visit to the beach was not on our agenda. An emotionally draining sweat gathered my shirt against the pasty mixture of dust and sunscreen on my skin. It was a disgustingly familiar feeling, but we weren't really thinking about our own discomfort.

A group of Canadians had come to the country for a cross-cultural adventure. They had run an energetic week-long day-camp for the children of the Pedro Brand community on the outskirts of the city. It was their last day there. They wanted to say goodbye by taking one last turn about the neighbourhood where they had recently become temporary residents. So, we visited people in their homes and asked if we could pray with them for anything.

Once we were done, we would leave the city and head to our debrief location. We would spend a day reflecting on the things that had happened during the trip and thinking about how to integrate the experiences with life at home. The team would leave the country, taking their experiences, new relationships, and bits and pieces of Dominican Spanish with them back to Canada. That afternoon would be the last impact on the memory of their time in the Dominican Republic.

Adriana, a former student who had been with the Dominican Team to Asia, had joined us for the day to help with translation.

As I explained what we would do, I could see the scepticism seep out of some students as they considered what door-to-door prayer might look like up in the North of Canada. A few raised eyebrows and suppressed smirks caught my attention, but they were genuinely trying to get into the thing despite the heat.

I couldn't blame them for their doubt. Evangelical Christians haven't really practiced door-to-door evangelism since the early eighties up home. The culture on the island is more open to the things of God brought to their door by unscheduled visitors. Saying so made a few shoulders loosen up, even if it didn't work to completely squash the scepticism.

We prayed and parted ways in smaller groups of three to six people, including translators.

The homes in the neighbourhood were formerly jail cells: cement blocks built for containing prisoners and outspoken political opponents to the government of Rafael Trujillo. Since Trujillo's assassination, the cells have been overtaken by displaced families. The hallways are dark and soggy, and the odd rodent scurries out of sight along cracks in the stained walls. Space is limited, possessions are few, but there is usually a friendly smile and an open door.

As we knocked on doors, some people talked for a bit, others welcomed the prayer. My group had covered a lot of ground by late afternoon, and we had prayed for many people. I don't recall a single door-in-the-face incident. Time was getting on. We had to meet up with the rest of the group and head back into the city before dark.

Once we regrouped, a couple of students immediately began to talk about their visits with enthusiasm. The scepticism had evaporated in light of reality. They had been encouraged, even though they were supposed to be bringing encouragement to the people. It was all backwards, but they agreed that it somehow seemed right. They discovered the gift of the visit worked both ways. Most students admitted that they didn't think anyone would talk to them and definitely didn't expect that anyone would welcome them into their homes, but *La Cuarenta* isn't Brampton.

Steven was quiet until Jorge asked him to tell the others about the girl they visited. He didn't seem to know where to start. He was stumbling over his words, trying to make the surreal experience tangible. He told our group that they had visited a sick girl in her home. With emotion, he explained that the girl had tried to kill herself sometime in the recent past, and right there during their visit in her home, she asked them to pray for her. In Steven's prayer, she received God's love for the first time, though she had heard things about God all her life.

Steven was emotional, still wondering about what he had just experienced. He was quiet. It took him some time to internalise and articulate the experience. He was awed that what he had hesitantly hoped and expected for the trip had actually happened.

That moment in the Spring of 2012 changed Steven's life.

In the lobby of the church where we had met for the winter retreat, Steven sat across from me and returned to that hot Spring day in Pedro Brand. His memories were fresh and agreed that the encounter still had great implications in his life. He told me the story as he remembered it:

"Juanita was about twenty," he began. "I can't remember if she had children or not, but it seemed that she did. Actually, I think she was pregnant. Her mum was there. She was young, but you could tell she had been through so much already. She had struggled. It seems to be something that is normal for that culture."

He looked at me wondering. His eyes begged the question: did I think that was something I considered to be normal in that culture? I didn't say anything but nodded vaguely, listening, non-committal. Many people suffer for different reasons. The people in *La Cuarenta* suffer for all of the reasons you can possibly imagine and some that you cannot.

"The house was different from most of the cells," Steven continued. "It was like a long strip," he drew the room with his hands, his arms stretching out to the sides. "The back wall seemed to be broken; there was light streaming in from the back. It was the last house in the row." He paused. "They seemed to be the last people on the planet." He let out a slow sigh.

"We were talking to her about life. We were sharing about God and then she just broke down, crying. She said she wanted to kill herself. Her mother told us that she had tried to do it before," Steven's eyes were wet as he remembered. The moment was right there with us as Steven talked. I could picture the situation. The contrasting cold surrounding us at the snow camp retreat could not hinder such a strong memory.

"Jorge put his arm around her and started to pray for her," he said. "She said she had no friends. Her friends had bullied her. She had nothing to live for. She just wanted to die."

Steven looked right at me, "You know, I was never really that confident in who I was in high school. In some ways, I could really relate to her and I really felt like we understood each other in that moment. I told her about how I felt, too." Steven had been sixteen at the time of the visit. It was amazing to him that a sixteen year old boy, young in the experience of life, could have anything at all to give to someone in Juanita's situation, but there it was.

"We get let down by people because that is what people do. Even your mother, friends, family — we let each other down. It's just who we are," he looked down at the carpet, the heaviness of that reality still with him. Then he popped his head back up and there was a corner of a smile on his lips. "But you know, God will always be there for us. I told her that and then I prayed for her, too.

"She was silent. She seemed broken. Just looking at this girl, you could see the emotional pain on her face.

"Living in that place, you're not really set up for success, but she had nothing on top of nothing. That was tough to see." He paused for a moment, seeming to remember the feeling of humility that came with being in that environment for a time, but living a separate reality in a different world.

"I felt like, even though I was exhausted from the lack of sleep and the travelling and everything, I felt like that moment was worth it. You know?"

He looked at me as if I knew what he meant and why wouldn't I? He needed to say it, though:

"I felt God's presence in that room."

That was definitely a worthwhile moment.

"Sometimes, they play cheesy music and stuff at churches to evoke an emotional response or whatever, but here we were, sitting in this jail cell with someone who was kicked down by life so hard and so far, and you just couldn't manufacture a moment in that place. There was no possible way you could manipulate the feeling of the presence of God in there. No. This was real. It was the real presence of God."

Steven disappeared for a moment and was back in that jail cell, surrounded by the dim lighting and the unbreakable poverty and the all-encompassing real presence of God.

"I kind of walked away from that thinking: Wow, that just happened …"

I couldn't help but show confusion on my face, "What do you mean? What just happened?"

"Well, when we signed up for the trip, we wanted *something*, you know? We had no idea what we were going to get," Steven confessed, dragging the rest of his team into agreement with his thoughts.

"I think," he continued, "a huge part of the impact for me was, well — living in Brampton, there is kind of this feeling that in as long as it takes me to drive to Toronto, I can drive out to the country just as easy. The feeling I got there was like: I can drive to a massive IKEA or drive just as far to complete poverty. That was crazy to me. Santo Domingo reminded me of Toronto. It was normal, it was like home, but then, right there, was all that poverty and hurt. All our expectations were kind of thrown out of the window.

"In training, we kept on saying: Alright guys, don't be expecting everyone to convert and stuff, but we were also saying that we should have big expectations of God. We were hoping for it, even if we were trying to be realistic in that hope. So, we kind of all had our own expectations about the trip and about God.

"At first it was a bit touristy, especially where we were staying. When we did that kids' programme, it was good. We knew the kids were poor, but the programme was really no different than a kids' camp at home, but then we visited their homes," Steven stopped for a moment, the thought caught in his throat, a crack breaking his voice. After a few seconds, he found it again and went on.

"I thought: Holy crap, people are literally living in prison cells where a dictator ruled, horribly. At this one place, there was no other light than one candle, no electricity, nothing. That's when it really hit me: this is their reality."

He stopped talking, the impact of his own reality choking him up again.

"What do you take away from that experience about the people, and the environment?" I asked, trying to help him find his mental footing.

"We all experience God in a different way," he observed carefully, finding a theological focus. "I was young, and I had only experienced God in one way up to that point in my life," he admitted.

"Something I took away was that no matter how poor they were or what their life was like, we all still experience God. The truth of God remains the same, but we apply it to our lives according to our situation.

"Applying Christian principles to my life in Brampton is really different than how I did during that time, and to how those people might as they live there. It was really something I wasn't used to. The main message is that no matter where we are from, we're all completely broken. That's the idea of redemption and grace. It's hard for me to talk about, because as she was vulnerable in her brokenness, in that moment, I felt broken.

"Here, in Canada, we can make ourselves feel safe, but in that moment, I became vulnerable. I hurt with her. There were a lot of times I've felt sorry for people, but in that moment, I didn't feel sorry for her," Steven's eyes filled up again. "I loved her. She is broken. She is a child of God, just like me. Just because I have better stuff than she does ..." he shook his head and looked at the floor. "We are still just as equally broken. Me saying that I'm better than her because of my stuff is ridiculous, because we are exactly the same. In that, we can begin to see the concept of grace," he drew out the theological truth.

I found myself awed by this eighteen year old in his honesty. He had grown up so much in the two years since the experience.

"It was a moment where I felt totally open, bared ..." his words trailed off and he played with the straw of his frozen cappuccino. I wondered at whether or not he really had travelled back by memory to the extreme heat of that moment; he was guzzling a frozen cappuccino in the cold of winter.

"You know," he paused, ready to throw one last thing in my direction before disappearing into the throng of youth at the retreat. "This isn't something I think about every day, but it forever changed how I make decisions; it changed who I am. It was a glimpse of euphoria; a timeless moment that spills over into the rest of my life. Up until that time, I made decisions based on the reality I knew. Now, after that experience, there is this new reality in my life. It was a game changing moment ..."

As Steven left the table to find his friends, I was left to consider the impact of cross-cultural educational experiences on the lives of students. There is nothing that speaks louder than the experience itself. They realise there is only one reality: the one that reveals all humans as equals on this earth in our tragedies and brokenness, and our collective anguished need for God. They know that the only reality worth living is one where we are participants in sharing God's love, which rescues and restores us equally to him. Subsequently, they've made their lives about that. They have a youthful spark full of limitless potential that aches to make the truth known.

They inspire me. As I listen to their burning passion to spread God's love, some fond and powerful memories surface. My memories chase me down and gird me in hope. I begin to remember. I see faint pinprick glints of radiance flash in the grey that has overwhelmed me.

The ashes are stirring.

It Circles Back to Asia

The more I think about reaching people from my own brokenness and about sharing God's love in this hurting world, the more my heart is full of Asia. Asia is where it all began when I first read *God's Adventurer* and became intricately connected to the life and mission of J. Hudson Taylor. Asia is peppered throughout my travels, wherever they have taken me, and Asia dominates four years of fond mission memories. Whenever people ask me about the greatest need for evangelism in the world, I spew relentlessly about Asia.

Asia is where it all circles back to in my life.

Over this year of recovery from complete burn out, the layers of my life's adventures and many passions have been pulled back to reveal what truly lies at the centre of my being: a delicate glowing ember. It's still there.

When I was in university, I was weird. I look back at that weirdo with admiration, though. As hard as I try, I cannot seem to write poetry quite the way I did in those convicted and conflicted late-teens and early twenties. I filled my days with hours of prayer and song writing, jaunts in the stark, cold hills of Northern Scotland, tea time with friends at two in the morning, and a passion for life and God that now makes me jealous of the me I once was. Weird and all.

There is a character in JRR Tolkien's *The Silmarillion* known as Tintallë, kindler of stars. Before I had a chance to get a rare copy of the book and read it, some of my equally wonderfully weird university friends began to call me "Tintallë" or "Kindler" as a nickname. Some would even refer me to others as "The Kindler" as though it were my official title. I didn't understand the reference until brother Jeremiah explained the Tintallë of Tolkien's world.

I was humbled. They saw something in me I hadn't noticed of myself: I am a kindler of young stars; I ignite spiritual fires and send those little stars flashing across this earth to shine for God. In missionary circles, they call that being a mobiliser.

In writing about my journey through the disaster of burn out, I have come to understand that though I was down for a good while, God has not yet put out my fire. (Hallelujah.)

Life has changed me; my wounds and scars will forever be the cracks in my human vessel that let God's light shine through, but I am not finished until he declares his work in me complete.

As I discover glowing embers — a desire to make the love of God and freedom in Christ known to the world — beneath the ashes, I am stirred to inspire young people to missions, to take great steps of faith toward sharing that love with the world beyond their current borders. Mostly, I try to fire them up for missions in places where the love of God has not yet reached.

All temporal injury, earth-bound pain and debilitation fades as I consider the eternity which lies ahead. I am excited for the next chapter of life. In contemplation of the next chapter, I have to admit that my heart turns back to the least reached masses; my heart turns back to Asia.

A HEART FOR ASIA IN LATIN AMERICA

I used to have a thick carmine anthology of people groups of the Buddhist world in my possession. I prayed for the young novice monk in the photo on the front cover, and the million people represented in the pristine pages. When I packed to leave Latin America, I was already over my weight limit for travel and the heavy book was taking up space. A thought occurred to me: during my time in Latin America my heart for Asia had not only increased, but had become contagious. I knew Dominicans who were on the path to go to Asia as missionaries, and others who led prayer groups for the peoples of Asia. The book, and the prayer it inspired, would not be neglected if it stayed on the island.

I left the book in the hands of Elizabeth. Her heart senses a fierce pull toward the people of Asia. She has envisioned one day being a missionary in Asia. The obstacles that stand in her way are almost worthy of being deemed impossible, but we don't believe in impossibilities. Challenges, certainly.

Her particular challenges exist in the intertwined bland realities of life that could paralyse anyone with a similar calling. She could live in mediocrity, choose self-advancement, self-preservation, and blithe comfort over the risky pursuit of Giving Her All for the gospel-centred dream. She could live oblivious, unaware that the common things of life cause immobility. She could smoulder the spark and douse the flame without even knowing. The demands of reality can strangle a passionate dedication to a higher calling. It would be easy to succumb to belief in impossibilities.

Elizabeth doesn't feel restricted by the obstacles. She knows that a day will come for action. Most days, she does at least *something* purposeful in light of her vision, like cooking Thai food for dinner or doing her shopping in the nearby Chinatown. She does the same things we all do: cares for parents, invests time and finances into a quality education, deciphers the right partner (if any) for her journey.

Elizabeth allows the idea of risking everything for missions to dance wildly on the fringe of her normal days, pricking every ordinary act and event with the thought of how these things might look different when she takes the plunge. Until then, she fans a flame, one that grows internally and spreads to others.

She prays and tells others about the need in Asia to share God's love and the truth of Jesus Christ. She inspires many in their search for meaning in life. She speaks with people who know their origin lies in the hands of a Creator God and those who know that their destiny is to be with their Creator God again at the end of life. She nudges them toward engaging in partnership with that Creator God to achieve a greater purpose. She even speaks with those who have been deceived by an earthly substance, veered from designed purpose, and have become ensnared in the tentacles of weighty material stuff. She embarks on a mission here and now to capture their attention and remind them of their true purpose: to be love and truth in the midst of many who yet do not know of origin and destiny, and therefore lack purpose.

Elizabeth accepted the hefty book gratefully.

It was never my deliberate intention to move the hearts of Latin Americans toward the harvest in Asia. Stuff happens to us along the way because of who we are and where we live. We be true to ourselves, and God stirs up the rest as he wills.

People started telling me about Chinatown outreaches and Chinese diaspora ministries popping up as far as neighbouring cities three hours away. I never went with those outreach or evangelism teams. It was all Dominican calling and Dominican work. I was too far gone on my downward spiral to add any new outreach activities to my schedule. At the time, I was preoccupied with transforming into a smouldering helix of combusted human. I had no time for mobilisation.

The Latin American church is lively and dynamic. Latin America has been on the receiving end of missions for hundreds of years. When the Jesuits and Dominicans joined the original explorers, it was to bring the gospel message to the people they might find. Regardless of our opinions about their efforts and methods, the truth was communicated. Many priests were martyred for their sacrifice. The truth stuck over time.

Since then, the Latin American Church has spread across the continent. In most towns and cities across Latin America, there are churches on every street, no matter what title they post, the presence of the body of Christ is undeniably evident. Many Latin Americans would declare that as a continent — save for remote tribal people groups in difficult to reach locations — they have been reached with the message of the gospel. They have been evangelised.

That isn't an excuse not to go to Latin America. Believers still face persecution. Community needs are great. Poverty is rampant. The worldwide church *should* engage in sharing the responsibility of meeting those needs and bringing hope. There is a substantial yearning for discipleship, training, teaching, seminary theologians, instruction on outreach and evangelism and missions. Don't misunderstand, there is still a tremendous need for missionaries in Latin America, but a significant shift is beginning to take place among Latin American Christians; they sense a call to go overseas cross-culturally and to dedicate their lives to missions.

I cannot count the number of times I heard humble Dominican pastors declare: We have been evangelised and it is our time to rise up and send out missionaries to other parts of the world. There is a new growing missionary workforce just itching to get to the harvest. Many are already out there, with or without the stability of a Western sending organisation.

Asia is the largest populated continent on the face of the planet. There are 1.3 billion people in China alone, with tens of millions in surrounding nations. The majority of people in Asia have never heard about the love of our Creator God. They do not know the truth: that he loves us and wants to restore our relationship with him. They don't know the lengths he went to in order to make it happen. We call the telling of that story Evangelism.

Evangelism is not a political message. It is not revolutionary propaganda. It is not fuelled by cult control, though often is unfortunately confused with that kind of obsessive nonsense. It is the only message of spiritual freedom that throws off the chains of *religious* oppression in order to bring all souls together in harmony. It does all that through the person of Jesus Christ. It is a message of freedom, but insists upon respect for government authorities at the restraint of personal preservation. It is the message that finds freedom in the promotion and care of everyone else but Self.

Asia is the least evangelised continent on the planet. The message is misunderstood, misrepresented and overlooked in the shadow of larger philosophical entities that dominate the diverse demographic. If you hold up a map of the world and paint the evangelised portions green and the unreached portions red, they tell me that Latin America is as bright green as the hills of Ireland. Asia is a stark span of deficit red.

While I spent time in Latin America, that overwhelming statistic didn't change much. I started to tell other people about Asia. They listened. They wanted to know what they could do. They started to pray. Seven travelled with me in the summer of 2010. A few plan to go for longer. I don't know how, but I don't need to know how. That wise kindred, J. Hudson Taylor once said: "God's work done in God's way will never lack God's supply." I believe that, as do many future Dominican missionaries.

I can't wait to see more missionaries for Asia come out of Latin America. Until then, Elizabeth can keep cooking Pad Thai while she prays for more workers for the bountiful Asian harvest. I hope that one day soon, she will be one of those workers.

DENGUE DRIP: PART II

Sitting at the edge of the street on a short plastic stool, I gazed at an elephant, young but careful, as she made her way through crowds of people. Her teenaged friend straddled the space behind her head, skinny strong legs tucked behind twitching grey ears.

Elephants are fascinating animals. If I were to own a pet, an elephant would be my first choice. Sure, I've had fish in the past, cared for borrowed Guinea Pigs, and we had two camp hamsters one summer. I fought constantly with Scathan, the stubborn black cat from a fishing town in the Outer Hebrides of Scotland who thought my pillow was his personal grooming cushion. I've also lived with a few dogs. I mean, real canines. Some pea-brained and huge-hearted, others temperamental or hyperactive, a broad variety of personalities. I've even shared a bond with one or two of them in my time, surprisingly.

If I could choose any pet, I would definitely get an Asian elephant. African elephants are too unpredictable and aggressive. In my limited experience, African elephants are not as personable and friendly as Asian elephants. I should say that I have no professional experience that allows me to claim that as fact. I base my assumption on my bias for Asian elephants, and from what I know of them; they are passive, observant animals. They display a sharp intellect and a cooperative nature. They are gentle and sensitive, and most likely to live longer than their owners.

Alas, I could never own an elephant in Brampton. It is completely impractical. Too big. Too risky. Too much dust.

I felt like this elephant was trying to communicate with me. Her glistening black eyes looked straight at me as she passed by, picking her way delicately through scores of tourists, and then she smiled. Not with her mouth like a human being smiles. That would just be silly. Besides, she was chomping mindlessly on a mouthful of something. No, she smiled with her eyes. Sure, it might have been that a bright light caught her in the moment and she squinted, but it looked like a smile to me.

I smiled back and lifted a hand to her. She was being clucked forward, but on her way past, she flicked her trunk out toward me. She missed me by a good metre, but the gesture was there. Gentle, intentional, able to connect with one person who was willing in a sea of noise and movement.

That's a smart animal.

I finished my bubble tea, and Kim and I stood to go find the rest of the group. They were off somewhere galavanting in the dark of the night market. I suspected that many of them were doing last minute souvenir shopping as we hadn't any time for that during the last three weeks of intensity. We had only sat down for a few minutes to sit and think.

The current group was about to split up. They would head home to Canada and the United States. I would stay on in Asia. I was hoping to make a visit to one more place, but I would take that journey without a team. It would just be me and a couple of friends ...

*****

The humidity of the jungle was not the worst thing I could ever have experienced. No. The worst thing was definitely the looming threat that any of these stretching and stacked cylinders of bright green bamboo bordering our path, green reaching to the sky, green scattered between our steps, overgrown, whispering through the passing of a rare light breeze, any one of these might be a Russell Viper with an appetite for human flesh. We trudged on fearlessly.

The trek took us six hours into jungle territory, dripping with condensation and perspiration, alive and invigorated by the untouched beauty of nature enveloping us on our walk. The purpose: to meet with, to share and touch to heal, to listen and listen and listen, to consider, to carry burdens, to sit with a people who never receive visitors, whose voice goes unheard.

When we finally approached the village in a small clearing, mud-covered and bamboo-stilted homes placed closely together on the side of the soft cleft in the mountain, the entire community scurried out to greet us. There were tears of joy, sighs of relief, excitement, a great sense of anticipation in the atmosphere. The buzz was electrifying. The affection was draining. The need was overwhelming.

And the incredible hope was astonishing against the contrasting backdrop of complete hopelessness.

I immediately internally pinpointed my limited humanity (I am nothing, nobody), my brokenness (I could never fix myself), my utter inadequacy (this is too big, I am only one, I am so very small). I bowed with respect. I was inspired by their lives within minutes of stepping into their town. I reached out an arm and they drew me into their homes, their hearts, their problems, the experience of their oppression. In that moment, I was changed forever, again.

The risk was worth it.

I later read that the bite of a Russell Viper claims your life within two hours. We were ten times that distance from any hospital or access to the anti-venom serum.

Even knowing that, the risk was still worth it.

I sat for hours and listened in that community, and that somehow brought healing, a relief to all of us. I reached out and touched the sick and the dying, and that somehow encouraged. It is a mystery, but a very real thing, a very powerful thing over which I have no power, but I bow very *very* low to the one who does: the Creator who gives life and takes it away, shares in our joys and miseries equally, who was overcome by sorrow and suffering daily. I cannot take credit. A friend of mine reminded me that I am a servant, a student, a storyteller. That is who I am and this is what I do.

I cannot explain how and I do not know why our presence, our touch and voice, and our sharing make a difference, but I know this: that the burden of a life oppressed becomes the heavy responsibility of the one who knows of it, the one who has seen and touched and listened, the one who has freedom. If I do not speak out, their voice goes unheard and I am as guilty as a wicked oppressor.

One man stood outside his house, his face torn with concern and his eyes begging. As we walked along the path, he reached out and pulled us in, quietly and frantically, pleading with us to help his wife, his dying wife. She had the worst kind of dengue possible and it was sucking the life out of her.

She was seated topless on a stool in the centre of the mud-house, pale and colourless against the healthy bronze of her companions. Her thick black cotton skirts gathered in weakened veiny hands, large red orbs covered the paper-thin skin on her back, her ribcage protruded, her eyes yellow, tired and sunken in dark grey circles that spoke of restless nights, anaemia, and a fast approaching death.

He thrust a transparent plastic sack into my hands. My friend translated that he was hoping I could drain the liquid into her frail body, give her new strength and medicate her. He hoped I could heal her. I stared down at the gummy bag in my dirty hands, looked back up to his wife, her black eyes pleading with all she had left. I slowly connected with each of the people in the room. Some stood close to her, their hands holding up her bony shoulders. Others leaned against the wall, gazing at the new hope that had just walked in the door, the look of futility on their rugged faces.

I don't know how to insert an IV. I could kill her if I tried.

He whispered to me, distress evident in his guttural words. His finger wiped across the black script printed onto the back of the serum pack, pressing into the words and leaving dirty smudges on the clear packaging.

I don't read Chinese. It was written in Chinese and another unrecognisable language that was not even local.

He is illiterate in his own language. How could he even think to be able to read instructions in Chinese? Impossible.

He insisted that I must be able to do something.

His strong skeletal hand, thick with callouses, griped my wrist and I felt his desperation pulsing in his steady fingertips.

Please.

He pulled my eyes toward her.

Please. Look at her. She is my life, the mother of our children, my partner. I cannot sit by and watch her die like this. please ...?

I blinked back tears and felt the bile climb the back of my throat. I backed swiftly out the front of the house, retching nothing into the weeds at the side of the mud wall.

My friend was suddenly beside me, a smile on her face. She'd seen worse. She'd cared for the dying, concocted herbal treatments on words of tribal prayer, hoped ridiculously for the impossible and had seen it happen. She put her hand on my shoulder and chuckled a little. She could find the humour in the strangest situations, a quality I appreciate deeply in her.

I regained my stomach, one hand on the cool mud of the wall, the other full of IV sack held back my lengthy hair. I don't do well with needles, or sickness, hospitals or suction-cupped blotches of blood patches across malnourished ribcages. I would have made a terrible doctor. I can't even watch so-called medical television programmes without feeling a tingling queasiness spread through my nerves at the site of fake blood and concocted autopsies.

I handed my friend the bag of clear serum with a pathetically apologetic look.

She whispered in our common tongue: We put our hands on her, we pray. Her voice was full of confidence.

She chuckled again: Hold onto your breakfast.

Hilarious. We hadn't eaten breakfast in two days.

I nodded, wiped my mouth on my sleeve, and took a deep breath of the fresh mountain air. We slipped back into the house.

We explained our limitations and offered what we had: no silver, no gold, no medical supplies or capabilities, but we had the name of Jesus. He is healing, power, love, freedom, restoration, and eternity. They received that without hesitation, hope lingering on the coiling prayers that rose and fell with their throaty expressions, my whispered affirmations swirling like incense, drawing each observer to the centre of the room to touch and hold her, and to invoke greater powers of healing than that which could be confined to a one litre sack of serum.

The colour returned to her face. A tear fell down her cheek and she smiled.

I breathed relief, her flimsy arm between my shaking hands and she bowed: Thank you.

I inclined my head toward her: I came here for you, for this moment.

We left the house and followed a trail down a pathway to the house at the edge of town. A man with Down's Syndrome lives here with his four children. His wife died in childbirth last year.

What could we do for someone like him? Was there anything? Was he even worth the effort?

We came here to meet him. We came here for this. We walked silently and confidently down the narrowing dirt path toward his house, overgrown with bamboo jungle, smoke from a smouldering fire wafting up from his front step where a tiny girl, maybe five or six years old, was brewing something for dinner.

She saw us coming, smiled an elated toothless grin and bounded into the house with joyous shouts of our approach. She stepped back into the doorway, wiped her soot-covered hands on a once-white tunic and smiled her brightest, most beautiful smile. Then she held out her thin arms and pronounced delightful words of welcome to her home.

We stepped into a dismal interior behind her waving arm of a grand greeting. Her father was seated on a wooden stool with a baby in his arms. He leaned forward to greet us, to take our hands in his, to bow a respectful reception. The little girl heaved the baby from his arms, malnourishment showing in both children. Two other boys lingered shyly in the corner, streaks of black soot brushed across their faces.

He told us his story, not shying away from showing his heartache at the loss of his wife, but smiling tenderly at his four children: his blessings. They huddled at arms length around him as he spoke, cried openly and smiled joyfully, a short speech that covered a hundred emotions.

He told of young love, the perfect match for him, a special someone who also struggled with simple things and suffered greatly throughout her short life. He spoke openly about her death during childbirth. He had delivered his own children, right there in his home between the mud hard walls and the smoking fire pit. His young daughter had assisted in the latest delivery, but there was nothing that could be done to save his wife. The child had delivered breech. Giving life was the last thing she had done.

He cried. He thanked God for the life she had been allowed, the wonderful children they had been given, the time they had lived together. He was not bitter, though sad. He was not angry, but grateful.

I said nothing, just listened and tried to imagine his conflicted pain and joy. The little girl inched closer to me as he spoke, her scrawny body roughly bouncing and rocking the infant to peaceful slumber. She was staring at me, but that means nothing here. Whenever I caught her eye, she smiled.

She was not even ten years old, yet the weight of responsibility of raising a family was already heavy upon her shoulders. I will always remember her black eyes, bright behind loose coarse strands of unkempt hair that bore the amber evidence of malnourishment. I don't remember her name, but she has forever marked me with her face, her welcome, her whole little self that embodied great big courage.

From beneath the ashes, these embers burn with compassion for that little girl and so many like her. I long to share the truth, that they would be free, that they might know the peace and joy of being restored to the love of their Creator, of being found by the one who seeks to give them good gifts.

My heart rekindles the smouldering spark of my youth and burns with hope that many might be born again.

EPILOGUE

In 2013, while I was in Santo Domingo, I received a long distance call. It was Sami calling from the United States where he had received a scholarship to study and work. He was able to send money home to his mother. He was making friends and enjoying his new life. He was getting married. He hadn't forgotten about me, but it had taken him some time to settle into living in America.

I wiped tears for the first few minutes, though less than if I had been seeing him face to face, and I expressed how happy and full of joy I was for his opportunity. It was a real chance from God to work through the burden of grief to find laughter and joy again. Sami was healing.

We lost touch again after I returned to Canada to finally allow myself to heal. At first, I was afraid to make contact with any of the people I had come to love during that surreal chapter in my life. As time and mourning brought healing, my heart longed to know how things had ended up for Sami, Joujou, Gisette, and others that walked in my repetitive dreams.

I found Sami and we spoke again for the first time in a long while. He told me that he is doing very well in his new life, that his mother is well, though still in Haiti. Then he said:

"I was telling my wife what a gorgeous person you are. I will never forget what you did for me."

All I ever did was give him a ride.

Joujou found me and sent a message:

"I was glad to find you so I could thank you for all the help you gave me. I hope the good Lord watches over your every step and hope that you succeed in everything that you do. I pray for the day when I see you face to face so I can thank you in person. May God bless and protect you in life. I love you."

I had wondered if Joujou would ever recover from the trauma of losing her parents and sister. I had often prayed that she would find her way back to some semblance of normal life, but I tried to maintain a realistic expectation. I was shocked to know that she had even remembered me. After all she had been through, she had faith. She could have been bitter and empty, and that would be understandable, but instead she had faith, and she expressed gratitude. My faith is bolstered because Joujou has a voice and she speaks of love and hope.

At my lowest, overwhelmed with burnout, and finding that there was no way back to what I was before, these amazing encouragements came to raise me from the pit of ash where I had burnt myself down to nothing. It was good to sit there for a while and contemplate the grandeur of God and to know again that He and the eternity he offers are what truly matters.

Kind words came in an email from Adriana, who has become a dear friend since her graduation: "I don't think a single human being has challenged and shaped my perspective on womanhood and serving God as much as you have ... you taught me how real women serve Jesus. I learned I could serve God despite my attitude and personality, and even more, that he could use those things. I learned to serve God in my own skin."

I was amazed. I know myself well and I am no Jesus; that people see him in me is a testimony to his great glory; that he can use a train-wreck like me is a show of his grace and power. I hope they see Jesus.

Elizabeth is in the application process to become a missionary with an international organisation. In the midst of mundane tasks and diverse aggravations, she keeps her vision alive. She longs to take the love of Christ to the far reaches of the world. She longs for people to see Jesus.

And there are others, brave students who surround me every Sunday morning and Friday night, who encourage me that there is no lost passion for those who are infused with the Holy Spirit. There are only cracked and broken shells, imperfect vessels who carry the perfect message of hope to a hopeless world.

I pick myself up, but I'm not going to wipe off these ashes, because they tell my story. Fifteen years, a short span in a short lifetime, was enough to drain me and leave me wondering how it happened; I would not trade a single experience.

I have a hard time putting missions into a neat and ordered definition for this global generation. That's okay, I think the mission we have in life to share eternity in our hope of Christ wherever we go should absolutely bust out of the boxed terms we use to define it. I hope a church asks me to explain missions one of these days, because when they do, I'll show them my life and I'll tell them my stories. I hope that even at my lowest, they see Jesus.

ACKNOWLEDGEMENTS

Krystal and Thomas, thank you for being my primary readers and editors and for giving me the best nieces in the world. I'd have no one to kick a ball with in the living room, or jump on the couch with, and that would just look ridiculous at my age. Thanks to Gianna and Mattea, for being naturally funny, loving, and for looking forward to reading with such fantastic enthusiasm. You both are the greatest human inspiration for me to remember to grab hold of True Rest with my whole self.

Thank you to the all the people who have shared your stories with me freely so that others might be encouraged through your vulnerability. It is an excellent thing to be together in this journey of life with people like you.

For all the Dominicans, and honorary ones, who have become very dear friends: Thank you. For Friday night all-you-can-eat-BBQs, late-night movies, afternoon coffees, doing life as a cooking show, and those spontaneous trips to Las Terrenas: Thank you. I couldn't say that enough in one lifetime. I love you all very much.

Thank you to numerous prayer partners, and especially my church family, for keeping me on your minds and hearts through it all. I am grateful for the example of brothers and sisters who have already gone on to glory before us. For those of us still in the folds: We press on together. Without your incredible inspiration, patience with a hyperactive child, stalwart example, and persistent guidance, I would not be who I am today. You have been my prayer force.

A special thanks to Nadine Frew, who patiently helped me remember the timeline of events that were most dormant in my experience, and to work through the mud of my memories toward freedom and a future. It was a grey year and our Friday conversations were bright moments of hope I will not soon forget. You have been a missionary I look up to since I was young; thank you for helping my find my feet again me this year.

To my family: Thank you for your support through the years I have dedicated as a missionary, my ongoing career in post secondary studies, and the most amazing childhood anyone could ever ask for. I love you all very much and cherish the moments we spend in the in-betweens.

Of all the people I have to thank, the two who never get it but most of all deserve it are my parents, Wayne and Kathleen. They encouraged my sister and I to explore and discover all manner of wonderful mysteries in our faith, never discouraged us from expressing our absurd doubts, listened when we had whacky theological ideas, and when we lacked faith, they prayed us through until we were filled again. It's hard to thank the people you live and eat and fight and laugh with every day, but thank you for being transparent, honest, and almost always funny. This book is as much your effort and work as it is mine. You have always fuelled my dreams.

My Granda never stopped talking about his limited "four score and ten" earthly years. He constantly emphasised the eternity that really matters. He was a powerful influence on my decision to freely choose Christ in every situation. When he was on his way out, joking about finally putting the other foot in the grave, he made me promise that I would always be wherever God put me and to keep my eyes on eternity. A month later, I was in Kompong Saom, Cambodia when I got The Call. He kicked the bucket, Mum said, and I knew. I sat outside under a thatch and tin roof, barely sheltered from the pounding monsoon rains, and cried with the crackling cell phone pressed to my ear. I have lost dear people in my life and agonised over their loss. I was severed again, but this time it was different. I anticipated missing him, but my tears were overshadowed by joy in knowing that death could not hold him, sin no longer pestered him; he was finally free, alive with Christ.

My life is all for Jesus Christ, even when I forget that truth. I owe him every breath because he has given me life eternal; he has truly made me free.